Italian Cooking Essentials

FOR

DUMMIES®

Italian Cooking Essentials

FOR

DUMMIES

by Cesare Casella
and Jack Bishop

COURAGE
BOOKS
AN IMPRINT OF RUNNING PRESS
PHILADELPHIA • LONDON

Printed in China

9   8   7   6   5   4   3   2   1
Digit on the right indicates the number of this printing

Library of Congress Cataloging-in-Publication Number 2002100370

ISBN 0-7624-1397-2

Photo Credits:
© Corbis: front and back covers
Photos courtesy of H. Armstrong Roberts:
© Hersel Abernathy: pp. 13, 14
© Larry Fritz: pp. 3, 60
© Jim Graham: pp. 26, 87, 88, 102
© Huber: p. 50
© George Hunter: p. 25
© Eugene Mopsik: p. 8
© H. Armstrong Roberts: 74
© ZEFA: p. 128

Spot photos by David R. Prince

Designed by Matthew Goodman
Edited by Michael Washburn
Cartoons by Rich Tennant
Typography: Cheltenham, Cascade, Univers, Myriad

This book may be ordered by mail from the publisher. Please include $2.50 for postage and handling.
But try your bookstore first!

Published by Courage Books, an imprint of
Running Press Book Publishers
125 South Twenty-second Street
Philadelphia, Pennsylvania 19103-4399

Visit us on the web!
www.runningpress.com

Icons used in this book

 This icon identifies the most important skills involved in Italian cooking and explains how to master them.

 This icon highlights ideas so quick and simple that you save time and effort in the kitchen.

 This icon steers you clear of potentially disastrous mishaps.

 This icon highlights inside information, timesaving steps, and expert techniques from coauthor Cesare Casella or another Italian Chef.

 This icon alerts you to possible problems in executing a recipe. When possible, we provide solutions for fixing a dish if something has gone wrong.

Table of Contents

Chapter 1

How to Think Like an Italian Chef

In This Chapter

• • • • • • • • • • • • • • • •

▶ Defining authentic Italian cooking

▶ Structuring a modern-day Italian meal

• • • • • • • • • • • • • • • •

If you think that Italian cooking is nothing more than tomato sauce and tiramisù, think again. Italian cooking is one of the world's great cuisines, with a tremendous diversity of flavors and methods of preparation. Many dishes are hundreds of years old, and some have their roots in the Roman Empire. Although Caesar and friends couldn't phone for takeout, they still enjoyed grilled flatbreads not all that different from modern-day pizzas.

Italians have a strong sense of this history, but the rest of the world (and that may include you) probably doesn't. Despite what you may think, Caesar salad wasn't named for the Roman emperor. In fact, Caesar salad isn't even Italian; it first appeared in Mexico in the 1920s. Spaghetti and meatballs was probably invented in Brooklyn, and tiramisù isn't the national dessert of Italy.

Okay, so you may not know what's really Italian and what's just an imitation. If the food tastes good, who really cares about its history and pedigree? Well, the quality of Italian food prepared outside Italy often isn't very high. In fact, some so-called Italian food is pretty awful. For many people, Italian food is fast food, akin to burgers and fries. Like anything that becomes overexposed, Italian cooking has become a victim of its own success.

Ready for your world to come crumbling down? There is no such thing as Italian cooking. Until the late 19th century, Italy wasn't even a unified country. Tremendous regional differences still persist today. Local traditions, coupled with the varying availability of ingredients, has shaped dozens, if not hundreds, of different styles of cooking, or microcuisines.

In the 1970s and 1980s, many Italian restaurants in North America and Europe introduced "northern Italian cuisine" to their patrons. They banished spicy tomato sauces and heavy lasagnes; instead they showcased rice dishes and refined pastas with cream sauces. Although this trend helped break the notion of one single Italian cuisine, it confused a lot of people. It left the impression that two Italian cooking traditions exist—one from the South, which is based on tomatoes and olive oil, and another from the North, where butter, cream, rice, homemade pasta, and polenta are king. Although you can find some truth in this generalization, it vastly oversimplifies the true nature of modern Italian cooking.

The Venetians eat quite differently from the Milanese. Both cities are in northern Italy, no more than a few hours apart by train. But the cuisines differ quite a bit. Milan is inland, near agricultural areas that produce rice, corn, and other grains. It's a wealthy city with a long history of meat cookery. Venice rests on the water, so seafood plays a major role in most meals. Venice also served as a crossroads for trade for centuries. You can still detect Mediterranean and Middle Eastern influences in local Venetian cooking today. Even dishes common to both cuisines are often prepared differently. For example, Venetians tend to prepare a creamier, looser risotto, with grains floating in a sauce of cheese and butter. In Milan, the consistency is firmer and stickier.

This is just one example of the regional differences that still abound in modern Italian cooking. Italy has 20 regions, each with its own distinct personality and traditions. Sicily, for example, has a warm Mediterranean climate that supports the growth of citrus fruits. The island endured numerous invasions and immigrations of people from Greece and North Africa. Couscous, chiles, olives, and capers became important ingredients.

In north-central Italy, the state of Tuscany has a very different climate and topography. And even within Tuscany, there are important distinctions in cooking styles from the coast to the mountainous interior regions. Urban areas, such as Florence and Siena, have their own culinary traditions, many of which date back to the Renaissance.

The Italian meal is a celebration. Tradition dictates that the meal should take at least an hour or two to enjoy. It's a leisurely process, with several distinct courses. The meal, usually eaten at midday, gives families a chance to talk. Eating becomes a communal activity—a time to share news of the day while enjoying the fruits of the cook's labor.

To some extent, modern life has taken its toll on this tradition. Italians compete in a world economy, which means shorter lunches to keep up with developments in New York, Tokyo, or London. And while most Italians are holding fast to their culinary traditions, more and more young Italians are trying things like microwaved dinners and American fast food.

But tradition still remains, especially on weekends and holidays. Even during the week, many people go home for long lunches, and most business comes to a halt in the early afternoon, only to reopen again around three or four.

Assembling a menu

The structure of an Italian meal ensures that the meal is well balanced. No single component dominates. (Italians are aghast at the notion of serving each person a 12-ounce steak.) The pacing is leisurely so that you can fully enjoy and digest your food. The five-course meal also allows for a good balance of flavors, textures, and colors.

When assembling a menu, keeping all these things in mind is important. You don't want to serve mushroom toast as an antipasto, mushroom risotto as a primo, and then grilled mushrooms as a contorno, unless, of course, you were preparing a special mushroom harvest menu. The Italian chef thinks seasonally and also works with the available ingredients to achieve a varied menu that's still easy to prepare.

A sample menu in fall may look like this:

- ✔ **The antipasto:** Mushrooms look wonderful at the market but are very expensive, so maybe you buy just a little and serve on toast.

- ✔ **The primo:** You can continue the autumnal theme with squash-filled ravioli.

- ✔ **The secondo:** Because the ravioli are fairly rich, serving a simple secondo, maybe a roast loin of pork without any sauce, makes sense.

- ✔ **The contorno:** So far, you've served nothing green, so choose a contorno like Swiss chard or spinach that complements the pork but also rounds out the entire menu.

- ✔ **The dolce:** If you are choosing a fruit dessert, think apples or pears rather than strawberries. A nut dessert would also work fine in this menu.

Planning a traditional Italian meal is like putting together a jigsaw puzzle. Start with the facts that you can't change, such as your budget, the number of people coming to dinner, the amount of time you can devote to cooking, or the availability of ingredients. These facts are the corner pieces of the puzzle, the ones you should put into place first. Perhaps you have a lot of tomatoes sitting on the counter, and they're looking very ripe. Or maybe you want to keep things light and avoid dishes with cream or butter. Next, you can start playing with the other components of the meal, making them fit as necessary. When you've struck the right balance, the result is a culinary mosaic, attractive to both the eye and the palate.

Chapter 2

· · · · · · · · · ·

The Italian Kitchen: Ingredients and Equipment

In This Chapter

· · · · · · · · · · · · · · ·

▶ Shopping for Italian ingredients

▶ Using fresh herbs

▶ Picking out some unusual tools of the trade

· · · · · · · · · · · · · · · · · ·

In this chapter, we detail most of the key ingredients that we use throughout this book, except for vegetables, rice, and pasta—all of which we devote chapters to. Here, we focus on the building-block ingredients used again and again in Italian cooking, offering tips on buying, storing, preparing, and using everything from fresh basil to Kalamata olives. We also help you figure out what's important and what's not when shopping for Italian ingredients. In many ways, being a good shopper is the first step to becoming a good cook. Italian food is so simple that the quality of the ingredients really matters. If you do any Italian cooking, most of the ingredients that we talk about in this chapter quickly become essential.

Although Italian cooking relies on a wide array of sometimes unfamiliar ingredients, the equipment used in the Italian kitchen is fairly straightforward. If you cook at home, you probably already own the most essential pieces of equipment—knives, pots, pans, and cutting boards—that you need to make most Italian recipes. We tell you about some traditional Italian kitchen tools.

Beyond Armani and Gucci: Where to Shop for Italian Ingredients

Italians sure make shopping fun. What would fashion be without Armani and Gucci? Unfortunately, shopping for Italian ingredients isn't as easy as shopping for Italian designer suits, which you can find in malls across the globe. We often find ourselves scanning the shelves at a number of markets to find the exact ingredients that we need in the kitchen. Here are our thoughts on some possible sources.

- **Supermarkets:** The typical North American supermarket carries a fairly good range of basic Italian food products. Most supermarkets carry the important vegetables (garlic, onions, and tomatoes), herbs (everything from fresh sage to fresh mint in tiny plastic pouches, usually near bundles of parsley and basil), and olive oils. Some supermarkets may even carry a few Italian cheeses and a couple of brands of jarred olives.

- **Gourmet shops:** The prices may be high, but most gourmet shops have a better selection of extra-virgin olive oils and vinegars than your average supermarket. Gourmet shops are also good places to find two important Italian pork products: pancetta and prosciutto. If your supermarket doesn't carry dried porcini mushrooms or arborio rice, the local gourmet shop should. Many gourmet shops also marinate their own olives and sell them loose.

- ✔ **Italian markets and delicatessens:** Communities with large Italian-American populations usually have a couple of Italian markets that sell prepared foods. (You can pick up many good antipasti at these markets.) Most Italian markets also stock an excellent selection of meats and cheeses (some even make their own mozzarella). You may find some high-quality olive oils at reasonable prices. These markets are also your best bet for hard-to-find items like imported instant *polenta* or precooked and dried cornmeal.

- ✔ **Natural-food stores:** For vegetable lovers (and anyone who cooks Italian food should love vegetables), natural-food stores are often the best source for the freshest vegetables and fruits. Natural-food markets are more likely to stock local, organic produce and usually have a good supply of fresh herbs and grains, such as arborio rice, polenta, and dried beans.

Grate expectations: Cheeses for cooking and eating

Italians are rightly famous for their cheeses. Parmesan cheese is used the world over to flavor pasta dishes, as well as egg, rice, and meat dishes. When shopping for cheeses, here are some guidelines to help you:

- ✔ **Search for only fresh cheeses.** Shop from a store that handles the cheese properly and does a brisk business so that nothing sits around for very long. A wedge cut to order is fresher than a precut and wrapped wedge.

- ✔ **Taste everything before you buy.** Good cheese shops unwrap cheeses and cut off small slices for you to sample.

- ✔ **Buy Italian.** Many Parmesan and other Italian cheeses made in the United States, Argentina, Canada, Denmark, and Switzerland lack the full flavor of the original. Read labels, which usually cite the country of origin. If in doubt, ask someone.

You have hundreds of Italian cheeses to choose from. Most, however, aren't exported. The following sections describe some of the most popular and useful Italian cheeses. Some are sold in supermarkets. All are readily available at a good cheese shop or gourmet store.

Fontina

Real Fontina cheese from Valle d'Aosta in the far north is rich and creamy with a buttery, nutty flavor. This is a fine eating cheese. (You would never eat some cheeses as is, like ricotta or mascarpone—they're just for cooking.) Let it come to room temperature, and it becomes soft. Fontina never gets runny like brie, but it shouldn't be firm, either. You can eat Fontina as is, or because it melts so well, you can use it in sandwiches or pizzas.

Gorgonzola

Italy's prized blue cheese can be made in various styles. Sometimes Gorgonzola is dry and crumbly and has an intense blue cheese flavor similar to Roquefort, a popular blue cheese from France. Although this aged cheese is fine for nibbling, when cooking we generally prefer a milder, creamier type of Gorgonzola called *dolce* or *dolce latte*—"sweet" or "sweet milk." The texture is creamy, and the distinctive blue cheese flavor isn't overpowering. If you can't find Italian Gorgonzola dolce, you might try Saga Blue, a Danish blue cheese readily available in supermarkets. The flavor isn't as distinctive as Gorgonzola, but Saga Blue is milder and creamier than most supermarket blue cheeses.

Mascarpone

This Italian version of cream cheese often appears in desserts. (It's essential in the trendy tiramisù.) You can also use Mascarpone to enrich pasta sauces or fillings. The imported and domestic versions of this fresh cheese are all pretty good and are sold in plastic tubs. Mascarpone has a light, creamy texture and buttery flavor. Don't try to substitute American cream cheese. The texture is much stiffer, and the flavor is quite different. Mascarpone has a short shelf life, so pay attention to expiration dates when shopping and try to use the cheese quickly.

Mozzarella

You can find so many styles of this important Italian cheese that figuring out where to start may seem hard. The original mozzarella was made from the milk of water buffalo and was called *mozzarella di bufala,* which is fairly hard to find in Italy and downright scarce elsewhere. It tastes best when incredibly fresh (no more than a few days old) and doesn't ship all that well.

Most fresh mozzarella (the fresh cheese is packed in water, not shrink-wrapped) is made from cow's milk and called *fiore di latte.* The flavor is milky and sweet, and the texture is springy, yet yielding. You should eat this cheese as is, in a simple mozzarella, tomato, and basil salad or perhaps marinated in olive oil and served as an antipasto. When cooked, it loses some of its delicacy.

When buying fresh mozzarella, try to get cheese that has been made that day. Mozzarella starts to go downhill after a day or two, and after three or four days, it's usually not worth eating. The cheese should look white and have a fresh, sweet smell. If the cheese smells at all sour or looks dried out, go to another shop. When you get fresh mozzarella home, use it immediately. If you must keep it for a few days, refrigerate the cheese in a container filled with enough very lightly salted water to cover the cheese.

Fresh mozzarella is made by hand and is usually sold in large balls that weigh between half a pound and one pound. You can also find smaller balls, usually no more than an ounce or two. Look for words that indicate size, such as *bocconcini* ("little mouthfuls") or *ciliegine* ("little cherries"), when shopping.

Of course, most of the world relies on shrink-wrapped versions of mozzarella cheese that are rubbery and bland. Never use these cheeses in a dish in which you don't cook the cheese. We prefer fresh mozzarella in pizzas, but you can use supermarket mozzarella in cooked dishes. When the cheese melts, the rubbery texture is less of a problem, and if you include other assertive ingredients (tomato sauce and pizza toppings), you may not notice that the cheese has no flavor.

Parmesan

Parmigiano-Reggiano is the name given to the finest aged Parmesan cheese produced in the Parma area in northern Italy. Although you may balk at paying $12 a pound for Parmigiano-Reggiano, most recipes call for very little, and the cheese delivers a large impact. Freshly grated Parmigiano-Reggiano (don't buy pregrated cheese; it dries out and loses much of its flavor) has a rich, buttery, nutty flavor. It's so good that Italians often break off tiny pieces from a hunk of Parmigiano-Reggiano and eat the cheese with drinks as an appetizer.

When shopping for Parmigiano-Reggiano, try to buy small wedges (about half a pound is a good size for grating) that have been freshly cut from a whole wheel of the cheese. A whole wheel weighs at least 65 pounds and has the words *Parmigiano-Reggiano* stenciled on the rind. When buying wedges, check the rind to make sure that part of this stenciling appears —this is the only way to know that you're getting the real thing. You can wrap Parmigiano-Reggiano in waxed paper or plastic wrap and keep it in the refrigerator for several weeks, at least.

If Parmigiano-Reggiano is just too expensive for your budget, look for Grana Padano, an Italian cheese made in the same region but usually not aged quite as long. Although not as complex, this cheese is still quite delicious, and it often costs much less (sometimes half as much) than Parmigiano-Reggiano.

Pecorino

Pecorino is traditionally made from sheep's milk, although some manufacturers add some cow's milk to reduce the pungency or save money. In Italy, Pecorino is usually sold fresh or lightly aged and is served as an eating cheese. Young Pecorino isn't widely known elsewhere. Most of the exported Pecorino has been aged much longer. Like Parmesan, aged Pecorino is designed for grating, but it has a much saltier and more pungent flavor.

Most exported Pecorino is from the Rome area, hence the name Pecorino Romano. (Pecorino cheeses are also made in Sardinia, Sicily, and Tuscany.) Pecorino Romano is bone-white cheese that has an intense peppery flavor. Like Parmigiano-Reggiano, the words *Pecorino Romano* appear stenciled on the rind to make shopping for the authentic product easy. Many American-made Pecorino cheeses taste of salt and nothing else; you should avoid these American varieties.

Pecorino is best in dishes with assertive ingredients, such as capers, olives, or hot red pepper flakes. Pecorino also works well with vegetables like eggplant and zucchini. Pecorino is widely used in Sicilian and Sardinian dishes.

Ricotta

Like mozzarella, ricotta should be freshly made and consumed within a few days. It should be creamy and thick, not watery and curdish like so many supermarket brands sold in plastic containers. In Italy, local cheese makers produce fresh ricotta with a dry, firm consistency (akin to goat cheese). The flavor is sweet and milky. This cheese is so perishable that it's rarely exported.

In the United States, you can get fresh, locally made ricotta in and near urban centers with large Italian-American populations. This cheese shares many qualities with the Italian versions. These U.S. versions are especially good in ricotta cheesecakes and pasta sauces or fillings, in which the cheese is the main ingredient.

You can use supermarket ricotta cheese, but it's bland and the texture mushy and unappealing. You might try draining supermarket ricotta in a fine-mesh strainer for an hour or two to remove some of the water. This can improve the texture, but you can't really do anything to improve its flavor.

An ode to garlic and onions

Many Italian recipes begin by sautéing onions or garlic in olive oil. These two *alliums* (a family of vegetables that also includes leeks, chives, and scallions) provide the flavor base for pasta sauces, rice dishes, roasts, vegetable side dishes, and more.

Although many Americans fear that onions and, in particular, garlic give food a harsh, overpowering flavor, this rarely happens in good Italian cooking. Italian cooks use the onions and garlic like salt to help bring out the flavors in other ingredients. They are infrequently the focal point of a dish and should never be so prominent that they're objectionable.

You must use a light hand, especially with the garlic. Two cloves can make a pasta sauce delicious. Use eight cloves only if you're expecting vampires that night. Also, cooking garlic over moderate heat (not high heat—the garlic burns and becomes bitter) tames its flame and brings out its sweeter notes. You should finely mince garlic (smaller pieces cook evenly and are less likely to burn than larger pieces) and cook it until golden. Cooking also changes the flavor of onions. The harshness fades, and the onions become sweeter as they start to color. The darker the onions become, the sweeter and more caramelized their flavor. Only when onions are burned do they become bitter.

When shopping for garlic, look for firm bulbs with no green sprouts or shoots. When shopping for onions, pick up red onions for most recipes. Yellow onions are also used (especially in the north), but red onions are the standard in most Italian recipes. Unless otherwise indicated, recipes in this book use red onions, although you can use yellow onions with a slight difference in flavor.

Store garlic and onions at room temperature. They should stay fresh for weeks. To peel garlic, simply use the side of a chef's knife to crush the cloves and loosen the papery skin.

To prepare an onion for cooking, follow these steps:

1. To peel the onion, cut off the stem and cut the onion in half through the ends. Gently lift off the dry outer layers of skin.

2. Lay the halves down on a work surface. To chop or mince, make parallel lengthwise cuts, starting just in from the root end.

Keep the root end intact to keep the onion layers from separating.

3. Turn the knife so that it's horizontal to the work surface and slice through the onion, again leaving the root end intact.

For small onions, one slice is fine; larger onions require several slices to produce finely minced pieces.

4. Cut across the onion to turn out pieces of the desired size.

Herbs: The importance of being fresh

Dried herbs have almost no place in Italian cooking. Sure, Italian cooks use dried bay leaves to flavor soups and beans as they cook. And some Italian cooks may add a pinch of dried oregano to a tomato sauce as it cooks. But that's it. Otherwise, Italian cooks use fresh herbs. Why? Because fresh herbs taste a lot better than dried herbs do.

Fresh herbs have all their aromatic oils. Dried herbs are weak and often about as tasty as fallen leaves. If you have any doubts, rub a fresh sage leaf between your fingers. The aroma is intoxicating and immediately recalls the woods. Next, open a jar of dried sage. You can detect some aroma, but it's faint and one-dimensional.

Most supermarkets carry a half dozen or more fresh herbs. And if you do any gardening at all, we recommend throwing a few herbs in the ground every spring. It takes very little time, the plants require minimal maintenance, and you end up with a steady supply of fresh herbs all summer, at great savings. Put plants into the ground or in clay pots and make sure that they get a lot of sun and some water every day or two.

Pancetta and prosciutto

Many Italian soups, pasta sauces, rice dishes, and stews rely on small amounts of pork to add flavor and richness. Pancetta is unsmoked Italian bacon that's salted and spiced and rolled up into a log that looks like salami. When sliced, you can see spirals of pink meat sur-rounded by milky white fat. You usually slice pancetta thin (like other cold cuts). For most recipes, you want to chop it quite fine as well.

American bacon is an imperfect substitute because it's smoked. If you can't find pancetta, try cooking strips of regular bacon in simmering water for a minute or two to remove some of the smoky flavor. More and more supermarkets carry pancetta, as do most gourmet stores and all Italian delis. If you like, you can freeze pancetta in small packages and just pull it out as needed.

Prosciutto is salted and air-cured ham. Like pancetta, you often cook prosciutto along with aromatic vegetables, such as onions and carrots, to establish a flavor base. Of course, you can also serve prosciutto as is for appetizers or use it in pizza toppings. Prosciutto crudo is the standard product that has been cured but not cooked. Prosciutto cotto has been cooked, like a boiled or Virginia ham. Unless a recipe says otherwise, use prosciutto crudo.

Flavor in a bag: Dried porcini mushrooms

The porcini is a favorite mushroom, with a rich, earthy, meaty flavor. Italians enjoy this mushroom fresh as well as dried. In the United States, fresh porcini are expensive and extremely hard to find. However, most supermarkets and gourmet shops now sell dried porcini at reasonable prices.

Dried porcini come in small plastic packets, weighing between ½ ounce and 2 ounces. When buying porcini, look for pieces that are large, thick, and tan or brown in color, rather than black. If the mushrooms are thin and brittle with lots of dust and crumbled pieces mixed in, find another source.

To reconstitute dried porcini, place the mushrooms in a small bowl and add just enough hot tap water to cover them. When the mushrooms have softened (about 20 minutes later), carefully lift the mushrooms from the liquid with a fork. Because all mushrooms grow in soil, they can be sandy. Usually, most of the grit falls into the soaking liquid. which is why you use a fork to lift the floating mushrooms from the liquid, without stirring up the grit at the bottom of the bowl. As a precaution, run your fingers over the softened porcini. If you feel any grit, rinse them under cold water. If the mushrooms feel clean, don't bother to rinse them because the water can wash away some of their flavor. The porcini are now ready for you to chop and add to dishes.

The soaking liquid is extremely flavorful; you should never discard it. However, you need to strain the grit from the liquid. The easiest way to do this is to line a small mesh strainer with a coffee filter or single piece of paper towel. Set the lined strainer over a measuring cup and pour the liquid through. Carefully discard the filter or paper towel (you should see the sediment) and then use the liquid along with the mushrooms. If, for some reason, you have leftover soaking liquid, place it in an ice-cube tray in the freezer. When frozen, pop out the cubes, put them in an airtight container, and use the cubes to perk up the flavor of sauces, soups, or stews.

Tomatoes

Imagining Italian cooking without tomatoes is hard. "Red sauce" is almost synonymous with Italian cooking. Many people are surprised to discover that tomatoes originated in the New World and first came to Europe only after Columbus brought them back from the Americas. Eventually, Italians adopted tomatoes as their own, using them in everything from salads and soups to pasta sauces and pizzas. However, contrary to popular belief, most Italian dishes don't contain tomatoes.

Italians love tomatoes, but they hate bad tomatoes. Unfortunately, the tomato has been much abused in the name of progress. In order to keep our markets stocked with tomatoes 365 days a year, geneticists, farmers, and marketers have engineered tomatoes that look great but taste horrible. Most of the perfectly round, red orbs that fill supermarket bins are picked when green, shipped thousands of miles, and then gassed to turn them red. They are designed for the shopper who selects food based on appearance rather than flavor. We suggest that you buy local, in-season tomatoes for dishes in which you don't cook the tomatoes. If it's January and you live in New York or Toronto, please don't make a tomato salad with mozzarella and basil. Choose another recipe instead of trying to make this dish with tomatoes from Holland, Israel, Mexico, or a hothouse.

When we want the flavor of tomatoes out of season, we rely on canned tomatoes (at least they're picked ripe) or oval plum tomatoes, which are also called *Roma* tomatoes. Plum tomatoes are not as juicy as round (also called *beefsteak*) tomatoes and don't have as many seeds. Their flesh is usually quite firm (one reason we don't think that most plum tomatoes are worth eating raw), but they do add fresh tomato flavor and texture to cooked dishes. When preparing tomatoes, remove the *core*—the small brown patch at the stem end. You can then slice or dice the tomatoes as needed. When cooking tomatoes, we often remove the peel first (the skin separates from the flesh and isn't terribly appealing) by submerging the tomatoes in simmering water for ten seconds and then peeling the skin with our fingers. Summer tomatoes are often quite juicy, which can be a problem when adding them to cooked dishes. In some cases, we seed the tomatoes before chopping them.

Chapter 3

• • • • • • • • • •

Before the Meal: Antipasti

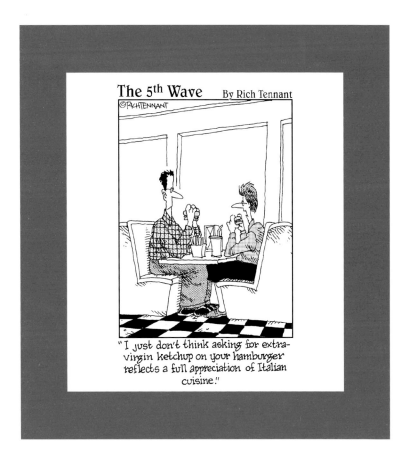

The 5th Wave   By Rich Tennant

"I just don't think asking for extra-virgin ketchup on your hamburger reflects a full appreciation of Italian cuisine."

In This Chapter

• • • • • • • • • • • • • • • •

▸ Defining the antipasto

▸ Making antipasti at home

▸ Selecting cured meats and cheeses

• • • • • • • • • • • • • • •

Antipasti from the garden

Vegetables are a mainstay in many antipasti, which makes sense in a culture that places such a high value on freshness and lightness. Many vegetable antipasti are marinated. The vegetable is cooked, dressed with a vinaigrette, and set aside at room temperature to marinate for a couple of hours.

Don't let vegetables marinate for too long, or they may become mushy. Marinated vegetables should be consumed the day they are prepared. Cover them with plastic wrap and let them marinate on the counter at room temperature. Marinating at room temperature also ensures that the vegetables are the correct temperature when you serve them.

Marinated Zucchini

In southern Italy, zucchini, eggplant, and even small fish are fried to seal in flavor and then pickled in a vinegar solution. The result is light and refreshing.

Italian recipe name: *Zucchine alla Scapece*

Preparation time: *15 minutes*

Cooking time: *15 to 25 minutes (plus 1 hour marination)*

Yield: *6 servings*

4 cups peanut oil

6 small zucchini, cut into strips roughly ⅛-inch thick and 4 inches long

1 cup red wine vinegar

Salt and pepper to taste

5 cloves garlic, peeled and thinly sliced

3 sprigs fresh mint

1 Heat the peanut oil in a heavy pot over medium-high heat until the oil is hot (about 350°). Add the zucchini in 5 or 6 batches, cooking until the strips are golden—about 3 to 4 minutes for each batch. Sandwich the zucchini slices between paper towels to drain very well and then transfer to a roasting dish or a serving platter with sides.

2 In a small pan over medium heat, combine the vinegar, salt and pepper, and garlic. Bring nearly to a boil and add the mint. Drizzle the vinegar solution over the zucchini. Marinate for 1 to 2 hours. Serve at room temperature.

3 You can also use raw vegetables in an antipasto. In the spring, Roman cooks pile baby fava beans, still in their furry pods, into a bowl. They place top-quality extra-virgin olive oil and coarse salt in two separate bowls. Everyone gathers around the table and shells their own beans, dipping them in the oil and sprinkling them with salt. You can also add a hunk of Pecorino cheese to this spread.

4 When choosing a particular vegetable antipasto, think seasonally. Often, the antipasto sets the tone for a meal. So, in spring, consider serving asparagus as an antipasto. In summer, peppers, eggplant, or tomatoes make sense. During the fall and winter, think about mushrooms, fennel, and leafy greens, such as spinach.

Vegetables with Hot Anchovy Dip

Bagna Cauda, which translates as "warm bath," comes from the Piedmont, where it is traditionally prepared in the winter. You heat garlic and anchovies in a mixture of olive oil and white wine to create a pungent dip for raw vegetables. The flavor is delicious but intense. We have a friend whose children refuse to go school whenever their father prepares Bagna Cauda. They think their hair and clothes smell like garlic, and they are probably right.

Italian recipe name: *Bagna Cauda*

Preparation time: *20 minutes*

Cooking time: *50 minutes*

Yield: *8 to 12 servings*

4 cups peanut oil

6 small zucchini, cut into strips roughly ⅛-inch thick and 4 inches long

1 cup red wine vinegar

Salt and pepper to taste

5 cloves garlic, peeled and thinly sliced

3 sprigs fresh mint

1 In a medium saucepan over medium heat, cook the olive oil and the garlic together for about 5 minutes. Carefully add the wine and cook at a low boil for another 5 minutes; make sure that you don't let the mixture come to a full boil. Add the anchovies and water and cook, stirring occasionally, for 40 more minutes or until the anchovies have dissolved into a paste. Skim the surface fat off with a ladle and discard. Season to taste with salt and pepper.

2 Transfer the hot Bagna Cauda mixture to a serving bowl, preferably terra-cotta. To keep the dip hot, set the terra-cotta serving bowl over a small flame or use a fondue pot. Dip slices of raw vegetables into the Bagna Cauda; celery, red and yellow peppers, cabbage, artichokes, cauliflower, broccoli, scallions, carrots, and fennel are the most common choices in Piedmont, but most any raw vegetable is delicious.

Portobello with Radicchio

Italians use fresh porcini mushrooms in this dish. Unfortunately, porcini mushrooms rarely make it out of Italy, so use meaty portobello mushrooms instead. You can roast or grill the mushrooms, depending on the time of year and your preference.

Italian recipe name: *Portobello con Radicchio*

Preparation time: *15 minutes*

Cooking time: *15 to 18 minutes*

Yield: *4 servings*

5 tablespoons olive oil plus 1 tablespoon for baking sheet (if roasting mushrooms in the oven)

2 tablespoons white wine

2 cloves garlic, peeled and finely chopped
1 tablespoon chopped fresh parsley, or
1 teaspoon dried parsley

1 tablespoon chopped fresh oregano, or 1 teaspoon dried oregano

Juice of ½ lemon (about 1½ tablespoons)
Salt and pepper to taste

4 large or 8 small portobello mushrooms, stems removed

1 head radicchio, core discarded and leaves sliced into long strips

1 Preheat grill to medium-high or oven to 375°.

2 Whisk together 3 tablespoons olive oil, the white wine, garlic, parsley, oregano, lemon juice, and salt and pepper in a medium bowl. Set aside.

3 Place the mushrooms on a plate and season with 2 tablespoons olive oil and salt and pepper.

4 Place the mushrooms on the grill or on a baking sheet rubbed with 1 tablespoon oil. If grilling, cook for about 3 minutes per side, brushing with the dressing mixture occasionally. If using the oven, brush the mushrooms with the dressing (to keep them from drying out) and roast for about 7 minutes per side. The total cooking time depends on the thickness of the mushrooms; whether you grill or roast the mushrooms, they should be lightly brown and tender.

5 On a server plate, spread out the radicchio and place the portobellos, either whole or sliced, on top. Serve the mushrooms drizzled with the remaining dressing.

How'd that mushroom get so big?

Portobello mushrooms are the darlings of chefs (because they look so impressive) and vegetarians (because they're so meaty). But where did these gigantic mushrooms come from? Are they on steroids?

Portobellos are nothing more than overgrown cremini mushrooms, another popular variety in Italy and now around the world. Creminis look like regular white button mushrooms, except they're light brown in color and have a much stronger flavor. If you can find creminis, use them as your basic mushroom when cooking. Like white button mushrooms, you should wipe creminis clean (or rinse under cold, running water if really dirty) before using them. You should also trim a thin slice from the end of the stem, which invariably is tough and a bit dried out.

When cremini mushrooms grow to much larger sizes, they're called portobello mushrooms. Each mushroom weighs several ounces (some even weigh half a pound), and the cap spans at least 4 inches, if not more.

Portobellos require some different handling. The stems are usually quite tough and inedible. You can add them to stock, but when grilling, roasting, or sautéing portobellos, trim the stems flush with the cap. Tender black gills cover the underside of the cap. To keep moisture in the mushrooms, try grilling or roasting them with the gills facing up, away from the heat source.

Sicilian Eggplant Relish

This recipe is one of Sicily's most famous dishes. You cook eggplant with other vegetables (in this case, onions, celery, and an assortment of peppers) in a sweet-and-sour tomato sauce that's flavored with vinegar and sugar. This version is lighter and easier than the traditional recipe, in which you fry the eggplant separately and then add it to the cooked vegetables. You can also mix this sauce into risotto or serve it with pasta.

You can serve this dish with bread or crackers for dipping, or your guests may eat it with a fork.

Italian recipe name: *Caponata*

Preparation time: *15 minutes*

Cooking time: *1 hour, 5 minutes*

Yield: *6 to 8 servings*

¼ cup olive oil

2 medium onions, diced

6 celery stalks, diced

1 small red bell pepper, seeded and diced

1 small yellow bell pepper, seeded and diced

1 small green bell pepper, seeded and diced

¼ cup sugar

5 tablespoons red wine vinegar

2 medium eggplants, peeled and cut into

½-inch cubes

2 large tomatoes, diced

1½ cups water

1 cup pitted black olives

2 tablespoons chopped capers, drained

2 tablespoons chopped fresh basil, or 2 teaspoons dried basil

2 tablespoons chopped fresh parsley, or 2 teaspoons dried parsley

Salt and pepper to taste

1 In a large skillet, heat the olive oil over medium heat. Add the onion, celery, and peppers and cook for 10 minutes, stirring frequently.

2 Sprinkle the sugar over the vegetables and stir in the vinegar. Cook for 5 minutes, until the vinegar has been almost completely absorbed.

3 Add the eggplant and cook, covered, for another 15 minutes. Add the tomatoes and water and simmer, uncovered, for another 20 minutes.

4 Stir in the olives and capers. Simmer for 10 minutes and then add the basil and parsley. Cook for 2 to 3 minutes more. Adjust the seasoning with salt and pepper. Serve warm or at room temperature.

Olives as an antipasto

Olives are a common ingredient on the antipasto table. Occasionally, you use them to flavor dishes, such as Caponata. More often, you serve them separately in a small bowl.

Italians don't use canned or pitted olives. They serve the real thing, pits and all. We suggest that you put out a separate bowl in which guests can discard the pits. It's not terribly elegant, but pitted olives are bland and mushy and can't compete with the real thing.

To use olives as an antipasto, you can marinate them in olive oil and perhaps season them with crushed garlic cloves, hot red pepper flakes, lemon zest, or fresh herbs. Then you can serve the marinated olives with drinks. Think of olives as the Italian equivalent of a bowl of nuts.

We always keep a jar of marinated olives in the refrigerator. The cold causes the oil to congeal, so about an hour before we need the olives, we remove the jar from the refrigerator and let the oil return to a liquid state. (This also takes the chill off the olives.) If you're in a rush, set the container with the olives in some hot water.

You can buy several kinds of olives and marinate them yourself. Try to find olives in a variety of shapes and color. Note that olives can be either brined in a vinegar solution or dry-cured with salt. Brined olives are plump and juicy and are generally the better choice in most situations, including antipasti. Cured olives are wrinkled and look shriveled. They're quite chewy and meaty (almost like jerky) and very salty, making them better for cooking than eating out of hand.

Of course, you can buy marinated olives from a gourmet shop, supermarket, or Italian deli. Either way, the olives stay fresh for weeks, if not longer, in the refrigerator.

Asparagus with Parmesan

This is one of those simple dishes that tastes like it took a lot of work but is actually quite easy. Asparagus spears are boiled, oiled, and then baked with a light dusting of cheese. In some places, this dish is prepared with eggs. Before adding the cheese and placing the asparagus in the oven, break 1 egg on top of each bunch of asparagus.

Italian recipe name: *Asparagi alla Parmigiana*

Preparation time: *15 minutes*

Cooking time: *18 minutes*

Yield: *4 servings*

1 pound asparagus (about 16 pieces), ends trimmed, stems peeled with a vegetable peeler if asparagus is thick

3 tablespoons olive oil

¼ cup grated Parmigiano-Reggiano

Salt and pepper to taste

1 Preheat oven to 375°.

2 Place the asparagus in a large pot with boiling, salted water. Cook until just tender, 3 to 5 minutes depending on the thickness of the asparagus. Drain. Transfer asparagus spears to a large bowl filled with ice water and let them cool, about 2 to 3 minutes. Drain again.

3 Separate the asparagus into 4 separate bunches on a baking sheet (so that you can easily lift each serving from the pan when done). Drizzle the asparagus with the olive oil, sprinkle on the Parmigiano-Reggiano, and season with salt and pepper.

4 Place the baking sheet in the oven and cook for 5 to 8 minutes until the asparagus is hot and the Parmigiano-Reggiano begins to brown. With a spatula, transfer each bunch of asparagus to a serving plate. Serve immediately.

A toast to start

In Italy, many meals begin with toasted slices of bread. Stray slices of stale bread often get recycled into diminutive toasts that are rubbed with garlic, brushed with olive oil, and lightly topped with anything from tomatoes to chicken livers.

The bread doesn't have to be stale, but it should be grilled or toasted. To make garlic toast, simply rub a peeled garlic clove over the hot toast. The craggy surface of the toast pulls off bits of the garlic. For a mild garlic flavor, rub lightly. For a real hit of garlic, rub vigorously several times. You can omit the garlic, but it's a nice touch, especially with a vegetable or bean topping.

As with the garlic, the olive oil is optional. Many recipes call for drizzling the oil over the toast to moisten it. If the topping is already moist or has plenty of oil in it, you can omit this step.

If you choose to add the oil, we find that a pastry brush (or a clean paint brush) is best for even coverage of the toast.

A toast by any other name

Toast goes by many names in various regions of Italy. *Bruschetta* is the most common name, but the terms *crostini* and *fettunta* are also used. You can use all three terms interchangeably; however, you should be aware of some slight differences between them.

Bruschetta comes from the Italian word *bruscare*, which means "to roast over coals." Traditionally, Italians grilled all toast, including bruschetta, over a live fire. Of course, you can use the broiler or a toaster. Bruschetta is often cut from large round loaves of bread, but this isn't a hard-and-fast rule. When made with larger pieces of toast, bruschetta should be eaten with a knife and fork and may, in fact, become a light meal, especially if you serve it with salad.

Crostini, literally "little crusts" or "toasts," is generally cut from baguettes or other narrow loaves and is rarely more than 2 inches in diameter. Crostini is always an appetizer, eaten out of hand along with a drink. Crostini is similar to the French canapé.

Fettunta translates as "oiled slices." Residents of Tuscany frequently use this term to describe this type of toast. Other more obscure names also exist, including *panunto*, or "oiled bread," and *soma d'ai*, or "brushed with garlic." Whatever you call them, these toasts make excellent antipasti.

Bruschetta with White Beans

Although we prefer to cook our own dried beans, you can use canned beans to make this recipe. Just make sure that you drain them into a colander and rinse off the gelatinous packing liquid.

Italian recipe name: *Fettunta con Cannellini*

Preparation time: *15 minutes*

Cooking time: *5 minutes (excludes cooking time for beans)*

Yield: *4 servings*

8 slices country white bread (Italian or French bread)

4 cloves garlic, peeled

2 cups cooked cannellini beans

2 tablespoons vinegar

½ cup olive oil

Salt and pepper to taste

¼ cup chopped tomatoes (optional)

1 tablespoon chopped fresh parsley (optional)

1 Preheat oven to 350°.

2 Arrange the bread slices on a baking sheet and place in the oven. Allow them to lightly toast for about 5 to 7 minutes and then remove the baking sheet from the oven. Rub the bread slices with the garlic cloves.

3 In a large mixing bowl, mix together the cannellini beans, vinegar, olive oil, salt and pepper, tomatoes, and parsley.

4 Spoon the cannellini mixture on top of the toasted bread pieces and place these bruschetta on a large serving plate or 2 each on 4 salad plates.

Bruschetta with Tomatoes

This dish is a classic summertime favorite. However, it depends on really ripe tomatoes. Give this recipe a try when it's local tomato season; otherwise, you may want to make something else.

Italian recipe name: *Bruschetta al Pomodoro*

Preparation time: *15 minutes*

Cooking time: *5 minutes*

Yield: *4 servings*

Special tool: *Food processor*

3 medium tomatoes, chopped

6 cloves garlic, peeled and crushed

12 whole basil leaves

Pinch of hot red pepper flakes

Pinch of black pepper

Salt to taste

3 tablespoons balsamic vinegar

3 tablespoons red wine vinegar

⅔ cup olive oil

8 slices country white bread (Italian or French bread)

1 Preheat oven to 350°.

2 Place the tomatoes, garlic, basil, red pepper flakes, black pepper, salt, balsamic vinegar, and red wine vinegar in a food processor.

3 Run the food processor for a few seconds and then shut it off. Repeat this procedure 2 to 3 times. The resulting mixture should be somewhat chunky rather than a smooth puree.

4 Add the olive oil and pulse a few more times. Adjust seasoning with salt as needed and stir. Arrange the bread slices on a baking sheet and place in the oven. Allow the slices to lightly toast for about 5 to 7 minutes and then remove from the oven.

5 Spoon the tomato mixture on the toasted bread and serve.

Roman Style Toasts

For this Roman favorite, slices of cheese are skewered along with slices of bread, flavored with a pungent sauce, and then baked just until the cheese starts to melt. Think of this as grilled cheese on a stick with garlic, capers, and anchovies.

Italian recipe name: *Crostini alla Romana*

Preparation time: *10 to 15 minutes*

Cooking time: *15 minutes*

Yield: *4 servings*

Special tools: *4 skewers*

7 slices country white bread (French or Italian bread), cut into 28½ x 2-inch pieces

12 ounces mozzarella, sliced into 24½ x 1½-inch squares

5 tablespoons olive oil

12 fillets of anchovies (about 1 can), drained and chopped

2 tablespoons chopped capers, drained

3 cloves garlic, peeled and chopped

2 tablespoons white wine

Salt and pepper to taste

1 Preheat oven to 375°.

2 Prepare the skewers by starting with a piece of bread and then alternating 1 piece of mozzarella with 1 piece of bread. When finished, each skewer should have 7 pieces of bread and 6 pieces of mozzarella (make sure that a slice of bread is at both ends). Place prepared skewers on a baking sheet.

3 In a small saucepan, combine the olive oil, anchovies, capers, garlic, white wine, and salt and pepper. Simmer for 3 minutes over low heat, stirring occasionally, until the anchovies dissolve.

4 Spoon 2 tablespoons anchovy sauce on each skewer and bake for 3 minutes. Turn the skewers and spoon the remaining sauce over them. Bake for another 3 to 5 minutes or until the cheese starts to melt.

Crostini with Chicken Livers

This classic Tuscan recipe can be made quicker and lighter if you like. Instead of dipping the slices of bread in chicken stock and then frying them, you can simply toast the bread slices and then spread the chicken liver mixture on top. If toasting the bread, cut the slices about ½-inch thick. In either case, you can make the chicken liver spread in advance and refrigerate it for several days. However, wait to fry or toast the bread until just before you're ready to serve the crostini.

Italian recipe name: *Crostini di Fegatini alla Toscana*

Preparation time: *15 minutes*

Cooking time: *35 to 40 minutes*

Yield: *8 servings*

Special tools: *Food processor, kitchen tongs*

2 tablespoons olive oil

1 pound chicken livers, rinsed and drained

1 medium onion, chopped

3 cloves garlic, peeled and chopped

1 sprig fresh sage

½ tablespoon flour

⅓ cup chopped anchovies (two 2-ounce cans, oil drained)

2 tablespoons capers, drained

2 tablespoons capers, drained

½ cup white wine

1 tablespoon chopped fresh parsley

Salt and pepper to taste

2 cups peanut oil

2 cups homemade chicken stock or canned chicken broth

One 10- to 12-inch loaf Tuscan bread (or Italian bread), cut into ¾-inch-thick slices

1 Heat the olive oil in a medium skillet for 1 to 2 minutes. When hot, add the chicken livers, onion, garlic, and sage and sauté over medium-high heat for about 10 to 12 minutes, until the livers release their liquid and it evaporates.

2 Add the flour, anchovies, capers, and wine and then stir. Cook for 5 minutes. Add the parsley and salt and pepper.

3 Puree the liver mixture in a food processor and then return the mixture to the skillet. Cook at a gentle simmer over low-medium heat for 5 minutes. Set aside.

4 Heat the peanut oil in a medium skillet until hot.

5 Pour the broth into a medium-sized bowl and quickly dip the bread in the broth; the bread should be damp but not saturated with liquid. Carefully place the bread in the hot oil for 2 to 3 minutes. Using kitchen tongs, check the underside of the bread; when the bread is lightly golden, turn it over. Cook for another 1 to 2 minutes and then transfer to a large plate lined with paper towels.

6 Spread the liver mixture over the bread slices and serve immediately.

The incredible egg

The frittata, an open-faced omelet that doesn't require any complicated folding or flipping, is a standard item on the antipasto table. To make a frittata, you lightly beat the eggs in a bowl with seasonings, pour them into a hot skillet, and cook them over gentle heat until the bottom is golden brown and the eggs are mostly set except for the top. At this point, you place the skillet in a hot oven or under the broiler to brown the top.

We usually choose the broiler for browning the top of the frittata. Although the danger of burning the frittata is real, this method takes just a minute or two. A hot oven takes longer (up to ten minutes), but the chance of burning the top is greatly diminished. If you're the kind of cook who burns food often (because the phone is always ringing or the kids are always fighting), go with the oven.

After the top is browned, you can serve the frittata immediately or allow it to cool to room temperature. The simplest serving method is to cut wedges straight from the pan. To get fancy, loosen the whole frittata from the pan with a spatula and then invert the frittata onto a platter. You can bring the whole frittata to the table.

A note about choosing a skillet: Italian grandmothers might laugh, but a nonstick skillet makes the whole process much easier and ensures that the cooked frittata comes out of the pan without tearing or sticking. Because the frittata will go under the broiler, choose a pan with a metal handle.

The seasonings can be as simple as salt and pepper, herbs, and grated cheese (usually Parmigiano-Reggiano). Most frittatas are a bit more elaborate and incorporate cooked vegetables. You can use other cheeses, especially grated Pecorino, as well as meats, especially pancetta or prosciutto.

The frittata is open to countless variations. Here are some quick, simple ideas. Start with 6 beaten eggs seasoned with salt and pepper to taste, a few tablespoons of grated cheese, and some minced fresh herbs if desired. Add any of the following ingredients alone or in any combination to the egg mixture. Then cook in a hot, oiled skillet as directed in the Italian Style Mushroom Omelet recipe.

- Chop and sauté several onions or shallots until golden.

- Chop several handfuls of arugula, spinach, Swiss chard, or other tender leafy greens.

- Boil 1 to 2 cups of bite-sized pieces of asparagus, broccoli, cauliflower, or green beans in salted water until tender and then drain.

- Cut 1 or 2 bell peppers into thin strips and sauté until tender.

- Cut several zucchini into small pieces and sauté until tender.

- Add up to 1 cup ricotta cheese for an extra-fluffy texture.

- Fry up to 1 cup bite-sized pieces of pancetta or prosciutto until crisp.

Italian Style Mushroom Omelet

This dish is equally good as a lunch entree or as a light dinner. Unlike a French or American omelet, you should cook the Italian frittata through. The eggs should be soft but not runny. You can serve this dish warm or at room temperature.

Italian recipe name: *Frittata di Funghi*

Preparation time: *10 minutes*

Cooking time: *25 to 30 minutes*

Yield: *4 servings*

4 tablespoons olive oil, divided

½ cup chopped red onion

3 cloves garlic, peeled and chopped

1 teaspoon chopped fresh oregano

1 teaspoon chopped fresh parsley

1 medium red bell pepper, seeded and chopped

2 cups sliced mushrooms (any mix of at least two of the following: domestic, shiitake, cremini, or oyster)

Salt and pepper to taste

6 large eggs

2 tablespoons grated Parmigiano-Reggiano (optional)

1 Place 2 tablespoons olive oil, the onion, and garlic in a medium skillet and cook over medium heat for 2 to 3 minutes. Stir in the oregano, parsley, and bell pepper and cook for another minute. Then add the mushrooms and salt and pepper. Sauté the mushrooms for 15 to 20 minutes, stirring occasionally, or until the mushrooms are tender and most of the liquid has evaporated. Let cool.

2 Preheat broiler.

3 In a medium mixing bowl, combine the cooled mushrooms, eggs, and Parmigiano-Reggiano. Mix well.

4 Heat the remaining 2 tablespoons olive oil in the nonstick skillet.

5 Add the egg mixture and cook for 2 minutes, stirring for the first minute, until the eggs begin to set. Cook for another 1 to 2 minutes, until the bottom of the eggs just begins to brown. (Lift the eggs gently with a spatula to check the bottom.)

6 Slide the skillet onto the top rack about 5 inches under the broiler and cook for 2 to 3 minutes, just until the top browns. Cut into 4 wedges and serve warm or at room temperature.

Antipasti from the sea

The antipasto course is a good place to use seafood, especially if you're trying to keep to a budget. A little seafood goes a long way as an appetizer. Grilled seafood makes an excellent summertime antipasti. Italians make good use of bivalves—clams, mussels, and oysters—in antipasti, as well as other exotic sea creatures, such as octopus and squid.

Purchase bivalves from a reputable source, and your prep time should be minimal. A quick wash to remove any grit from the exterior should be sufficient.

Octopus and squid require a lot of cleaning. You can save a few bucks and do this yourself, or you can ask your fishmonger to clean them. Unless you like handling slimy, smelly innards, we suggest spending the extra bucks. Squid and octopus aren't exactly flying off the shelves and are pretty cheap either way.

The biggest mistake that novice cooks make when preparing seafood antipasti is overcooking. Squid and octopus become tough and rubbery if you leave them on the grill for too long, and clams, mussels, and oysters dry out after just a few minutes of cooking. Read recipes carefully and watch the clock.

Peppered Mussels

This simple dish is among our favorites from Naples. Most mussels are now farmed in seabeds and come to market quite clean. Simply wash the mussels with a scrub brush and pull off any weedlike material that hangs from the shells. This part of the mussel is called the beard, and it's often, but not always, removed during processing.

Italian recipe name: *Pepata di Cozze*

Preparation time: *30 minutes*

Cooking time: *12 minutes*

Yield: *4 servings*

4 pounds mussels	*5 cloves garlic, peeled and finely chopped*
⅓ cup white wine	*¾ teaspoon salt*
¼ cup finely chopped fresh parsley	*1 teaspoon pepper*

1 Clean the mussels, removing the beard and scrubbing the shells with a clean scrub brush.

2 Place the mussels and wine in a large pot over medium heat and cook for about 10 minutes, covered, until the mussels have opened. Discard any mussels that remain closed.

3 Add the parsley, garlic, and salt and pepper. Stir to combine. Continue cooking for 2 minutes and then turn off the heat and set aside, covered, for 2 to 3 minutes.

4 Serve hot in large soup or pasta bowls with a side plate for the shells.

Broiled Squid

Fried calamari is a restaurant dish. At home, it's easier and less smelly to broil the squid. Make sure that you buy fully cleaned squid.

Italian recipe name: *Calamari alla Griglia*

Preparation time: *15 minutes*

Cooking time: *8 to 15 minutes (depends on cooking method selected)*

Yield: *4 servings*

½ cup bread crumbs

2 cloves garlic, peeled and finely chopped

½ tablespoon finely chopped fresh rosemary, or ½ teaspoon dried rosemary

½ tablespoon finely chopped fresh thyme, or ½ teaspoon dried thyme

½ tablespoon finely chopped fresh sage, or ½ teaspoon dried sage

½ tablespoon finely chopped fresh oregano, or ½ teaspoon dried oregano

¼ cup olive oil

1½ pounds squid, cleaned, cut into ¼-inch rings

2 medium tomatoes, cut into ¼-inch-thick slices

Salt and pepper to taste

1 bunch arugula, washed and trimmed

1 Preheat the broiler. If you plan on baking the squid, preheat oven to 375°.

2 In a medium bowl, combine the bread crumbs, garlic, herbs, and olive oil. Stir with a wooden spoon until the mixture is somewhat sticky.

3 Add the squid to the bowl and gently stir until all the rings are coated with the bread crumb mixture. Arrange the squid on a baking sheet and broil for 3 to 4 minutes per side until lightly browned. To cook in the oven, arrange the squid on a baking sheet and bake for 12 to 15 minutes, turning occasionally. Again, the squid turns light brown and becomes crunchy when done.

4 Arrange the tomato slices on 4 plates and spoon the squid on top. Season with salt and pepper. Garnish with the arugula leaves.

Stuffed Oysters, Taranto Style

Oysters are tricky to work with. Don't attempt to open oysters yourself; ask your fishmonger to open them. Doing this safely and efficiently takes years of practice. You can also make this southern Italian dish with littleneck or cherrystone clams, if desired. You should get the clams opened at the fish store as well.

Italian recipe name: *Ostriche alla Tarantina*

Preparation time: *15 minutes*

Cooking time: *15 to 20 minutes*

Yield: *4 servings*

6 tablespoons bread crumbs

4 to 6 tablespoons olive oil, divided

5 cloves garlic, peeled and chopped

3 tablespoons chopped fresh parsley

3 tablespoons grated Parmigiano-Reggiano

1 teaspoon chopped fresh thyme, or
½ teaspoon dried thyme

Salt and pepper to taste

24 oysters with shells (or substitute clams)

1 lemon, cut into wedges

1 Preheat oven to 375° or preheat broiler (oven rack should be 3 to 4 inches from heat).

2 In a mixing bowl, combine the bread crumbs, 2 tablespoons olive oil, garlic, parsley, Parmigiano-Reggiano, thyme, and salt and pepper. Mix well.

3 Pack the bread crumb mixture into neat mounds over the oysters in the half-shells and then place the shells on a baking sheet. Sprinkle with 2 tablespoons olive oil. Bake 15 to 20 minutes or broil 3 to 4 minutes until golden brown and crisp. Serve warm with lemon wedges.

Meat and cheese antipasti

Cured meats and cheeses are another important category of antipasti. An Italian deli, called a *salumeria,* carries dozens of salamis and cheeses, as well as prosciutto. Although the home cook can embellish these store-bought ingredients, for the most part, meat and cheese antipasti involve little preparation.

Italy produces literally hundreds of cheeses; most varieties never leave Italy. A small handful—no more than a dozen—are available internationally, and of those, only a few are commonly used as antipasti. Here's a list of our favorite cheeses to serve as antipasti.

- **Mozzarella:** Use only fresh, creamy, homemade mozzarella. Avoid rubbery, shrink-wrapped versions at all costs, especially if you're not going to cook the cheese. You can marinate tiny mozzarella balls, often called *bocconcini* (or "little mouthfuls") in extra-virgin olive oil that has been spiked with hot red pepper flakes.

- **Parmigiano-Reggiano:** A hunk of Parmigiano-Reggiano is perfect for nibbling on with drinks and olives. Use a short, broad-bladed knife with a pointed end to furrow into the cheese and break off irregular chunks. You should eat only the finest Parmigiano-Reggiano this way. You may enjoy good Pecorino in the same fashion.

- **Gorgonzola:** This is Italy's famed blue cheese. You can find numerous styles of Gorgonzola—from the creamy, mild *latte dolce,* or "sweet milk," to crumbly, aged versions that are quite potent and usually very salty. We generally prefer the milder, creamier cheeses when planning an antipasto.

- **Other creamy cheeses:** You can serve other creamy cheeses with bread or crackers. Italian Fontina has a mild, buttery, even nutty flavor. Taleggio is a buttery, sometimes runny, cheese with a rind—think of this as brie, but with a funkier aftertaste.

In addition to cheeses, your local gourmet shop or Italian market should carry a selection of cured pork products, including salami and prosciutto. A platter of cured meats is a commonly offered antipasto in northern Italy. You may serve these meats singly or in combination, allotting ½ to 1 ounce per person. Here are several possible choices; note that you can find dozens more.

- **Salami** is dry cured sausage made from minced lean meat and pork fat. The meat is usually all pork, but occasionally some beef is added. The meat and fat may be seasoned with garlic, fennel seeds, chiles, or even white wine. Salamis are cured for several months and sometimes up to a year. You can ask the butcher to slice the salami for you or simply cut it yourself into slices or small cubes.

- **Mortadella** is Italy's answer to bologna. Pork is beaten into a smooth puree that is light and airy. This pink puree is seasoned, often with warm spices like cinnamon and nutmeg. Mortadella looks like oversized bologna studded with cracked peppercorns and large cubes of creamy white fat. Mortadella originally hails from the city of Bologna. Although bland bologna takes it name from this city as well, mortadella is much more complex. Never spicy like salami, it nonetheless is richly seasoned and delicious.

- **Coppa** is cured pork shoulder sold in thick, short logs. The meat should be rosy-colored and well-marbled with fat. The meat is seasoned with salt and black pepper, as well as with an aromatic spice like cinnamon or nutmeg.

- **Bresaola** is salted, air-dried, and pressed beef that you slice very thin and serve with a drizzle of olive oil and lemon juice. Originally from Lombardy, this cured beef is popular throughout Italy now.

- **Prosciutto** is salted and air-dried fresh ham. Called *prosciutto crudo* in Italian, this product has been cured but not cooked. (The term *prosciutto cotto* refers to cooked ham, not unlike boiled ham.) Prosciutto crudo is not smoked. The flavor is simply the ham plus the seasonings, usually salt and black pepper. The butcher must slice the prosciutto paper-thin so that pieces melt in your mouth. Italian prosciutto from the Parma region is now available around the globe. It may cost a few dollars more per pound than domestic products, but it's money well spent. You may eat prosciutto as is or with fruit, especially melon and figs. (You don't need a recipe for this; just serve thinly sliced prosciutto with halved fresh figs or chunks of peeled canteloupe or honeydew melon.)

In addition to cured meats, Italians also enjoy thin-sliced, raw beef as an antipasto. Beef carpaccio is a common appetizer in Italian restaurants. Layer thin pieces of tender beef over a bed of salad greens, moisten the beef with olive oil and lemon juice, and serve with pieces of Parmigiano-Reggiano. The cut of beef must be tender. Filet mignon is a good choice, as is top round.

Raw Beef Salad

If you like, have your butcher slice the beef for this salad on his slicing machine. Tell the butcher that you're making carpaccio and that you need the filet mignon sliced paper-thin. The slices should be just thick enough to hold together without shredding. If you decide to do this yourself, put the meat in the freezer for 30 minutes to make it firmer and easier to slice. Then, after slicing the meat, pound the slices between pieces of plastic wrap with a heavy mallet or the bottom of a heavy pan to get them really thin.

Don't be put off by the number of different herbs called for in this recipe. Just use whatever herbs you have.

Italian recipe name: *Carpaccio*

Preparation time: *20 minutes*

Cooking time: *None*

Yield: *4 servings*

2 scallions, finely chopped (white part only)

¼ teaspoon finely chopped fresh thyme, or ⅛ teaspoon dried thyme

¼ teaspoon finely chopped fresh chervil, or ⅛ teaspoon dried chervil

¼ teaspoon finely chopped marjoram, or ⅛ teaspoon dried marjoram

¼ teaspoon finely chopped basil, or ⅛ teaspoon dried basil

¼ teaspoon finely chopped fresh chili pepper, or ⅛ teaspoon dried chili powder

½ cup olive oil

Juice of 1 lemon (about 3 tablespoons)

Pepper to taste

4 cups arugula, washed, trimmed, and dried

¾ pound filet mignon

2 ounces Parmigiano-Reggiano, shaved into thin slices

1 In a small bowl, mix together the scallions, thyme, chervil, marjoram, basil, chili pepper, olive oil, lemon juice, and pepper.

2 Arrange the arugula in neat mounds on the center of 4 plates.

3 Slice the meat as thin as possible; you should have at least 12 slices. Place the meat between 2 sheets of waxed paper or plastic wrap and pound with a meat mallet or the bottom of a heavy pan. The meat should be even in thickness (paper-thin). Drape 3 slices of meat over each mound of arugula and drizzle with the dressing.

4 Arrange Parmigiano-Reggiano cheese shavings on top and serve.

Chapter 4

· · · · · · · · · ·

Salads

The 5th Wave   By Rich Tennant

"What my husband meant to say is he made a 'Caesar salad', not a 'Cesarean salad'."

In This Chapter

· ·

▶ Marrying oil and vinegar
▶ Mixing and matching salad greens
▶ Taming bitter greens

· ·

Making a good salad should be easy, but not mindless. You may think that preparing salad means opening a bag of prewashed lettuce and tossing it in a large bowl with some bottled dressing. You can make salad this way, but will it taste great? Not likely.

Salad gets a bit more respect in Italy. It's still easy to prepare, but the quality of the ingredients is much higher. You won't find packages of "Italian seasonings for dressing" (which taste too much like grass) or bland greens. Salad shouldn't be something you eat to pass the time, waiting for the dinner to be served. It should have its own character and be packed with flavor.

A good salad begins with fresh leafy greens or perhaps some cooked potatoes, sliced fennel and oranges, or steamed mussels. The dressing can be as simple as a drizzle of extra-virgin olive oil and some good vinegar. Of course, you can get fancier by adding herbs, garlic, or other seasonings, but at heart, Italian dressings are ridiculously easy.

Two kinds of salads are popular in Italy—leafy salads and room-temperature vegetables, seafood, or meat dressed with oil and vinegar. Leafy salads are so simple that you don't really need a recipe. They're a place for improvisation and creativity, as long as you follow some basic rules about handling greens and dressing them. Room-temperature salads, with cooked vegetables, seafood, or meat, require more attention to detail. This chapter explains how to prepare both types of salad. No more salad from a bag!

The Marriage of Oil and Vinegar

As with most marriages, a dressing is only as strong as the two partners—in this case, oil and vinegar. In Italy, extra-virgin olive oil is the first (and in most cases the only) choice for salad. If you can afford a bottle of cold-pressed Italian olive oil, this is the place to use it.

Vinegar 101

Although the oil may be the flashy member of the duo, the vinegar is just as important. Here's a rundown on the choices:

- **Red wine vinegar:** The better the red wine, the better the vinegar. Imported red wine vinegar tends to be slightly more acidic than domestic brands, but either makes a dressing with a strong kick. Like wine, good red wine vinegar is full-bodied and complex.

- **White wine vinegar:** Less full-bodied than vinegar made with red wine, white wine vinegar is still fairly acidic. When you don't want a pink dressing (for example, a dressing made with red wine vinegar dyes cauliflower and other white foods), use white wine vinegar. Don't buy distilled white vinegar, which is made from grains, not wine, and has little flavor.

✔ **Citrus juice:** Many Italian salad dressings don't contain any vinegar. Before juicing lemons or oranges, think about grating some of the peel and adding a little to the dressing. The zest boosts the citrus flavor without altering the acid-to-oil ratio. If you can get your hands on some ruby red blood oranges, use them in dressing. Their musky, sweet-and-sour flavor and unusual red color are not to be missed.

✔ **Balsamic vinegar:** Balsamic vinegar has a rich brown color and sweet, woody flavor that comes from aging in casks. Many recipes call for half balsamic vinegar and half red wine vinegar. This ratio helps balance the sweetness of the balsamic vinegar and keeps it from overpowering other ingredients.

Balsamic vinegar

Balsamic vinegar is the trendy condiment of choice for everything from salad dressings to sauces. However, most Americans would be surprised to learn that they have never tasted "real" balsamic vinegar. Even more shocking, balsamic vinegar is more popular in the United States than in Italy, where its culinary uses are actually quite limited. Contrary to what the chef at your local restaurant may think, balsamic vinegar is not Italy's answer to soy sauce. Balsamic vinegar has very specific uses. One of those is salad dressing.

Many cheap brands of balsamic vinegar are simply red wine vinegar with caramel added for color and sweetness. If a bottle of "balsamic vinegar" costs $2, you can be sure it has not been aged and isn't the real thing.

While the real thing can cost upwards of $50 an ounce, a happy middle ground is available. Unaged balsamic vinegar is harsh and unpleasant, but aging for 12 or more years makes the product costly to produce. The solution some companies have adopted is aging for several years in wood. The resulting vinegar has a gentle sweetness combined with a low-to-moderate acidity; a complex, woody bouquet and flavor reminiscent of fruit; and a dense, syrupy consistency—all qualities that are revered in traditional balsamic vinegar. A small bottle costs $5 or $10, but remember that a little goes a long way. When shopping, read labels carefully. Vinegars that are aged usually say so.

Even quality commercial balsamic vinegars are not used straight in salad dressings in Italy, but are usually combined with red wine vinegar. Other traditional uses—such as sprinkling over steamed asparagus, sliced Parmesan, or vanilla gelato—require very small quantities. Italians do not generally cook with balsamic vinegar because heat destroys its subtle qualities. To use balsamic vinegar in savory foods, add a few drops to a sauce just before serving or drizzle some over a piece of grilled fish. So why does a 3-ounce bottle of traditional aged balsamic vinegar cost $150? The answer is low yield and high storage fees. A typical vineyard acre may produce enough grape juice to make 800 gallons of wine vinegar. After the juice from those same grapes has been cooked down and aged, during which time massive evaporation occurs, just 20 or 30 gallons of balsamic vinegar remain. High storage costs (just keeping water that long is expensive) add to the final price, which is rarely less than $60 per bottle and can climb to $200.

Making dressing

Like oil and water, oil and vinegar would rather remain separate. Put them together in a bowl, and the oil rises to the top and the vinegar sinks to the bottom. Use a colored vinegar, such as red wine vinegar, and you actually see the red vinegar layer on the bottom and the oil on top.

But mixing the oil and vinegar together is essential for making an emulsion, a scientific term that refers to any mixture of liquids that don't ordinarily combine. Salad dressing is an emulsion. The French call this cold sauce vinaigrette, and so does much of the rest of the world.

To make a vinaigrette, start by beating (with a fork or small wire whisk) the vinegar, salt and pepper, and any other seasonings (mustard, spices, and so on) together in a bowl until smooth. Drizzle in the oil and beat until the dressing is smooth. Use a light hand with seasonings—a pinch of salt and pepper is fine and a teaspoon of mustard is plenty. As for the amount of oil, use 2 to 4 tablespoons oil for every tablespoon of vinegar. Of course, taste the dressing (dip a piece of lettuce into the bowl if you like) and adjust the seasonings and amount of oil to suit your personal tastes.

Vinaigrette can be set aside at room temperature for several hours or refrigerated for several days. However, after several minutes, the emulsion breaks and the oil and vinegar separates. Simply whisk again right before drizzling over greens and the vinaigrette is as good as new.

The following tomato and cheese salad is dressed with Italy's simplest and most common vinaigrette, made with red wine vinegar, salt and pepper, and olive oil. This dressing complements almost any salad ingredients.

Tomato and Mozzarella Salad, Capri Style

This classic Italian salad works well as a light lunch or as an appetizer. This summer dish depends on ripe tomatoes, fresh basil, and good-quality fresh mozzarella cheese. You can add sliced red onions as well.

Italian recipe name: *Insalata Caprese*

Preparation time: *10 minutes*

Cooking time: *None*

Yield: *4 servings*

1 tablespoon red wine vinegar
Salt and pepper to taste

2 tablespoons olive oil

2 cups arugula, washed (optional)

2 large ripe tomatoes, cut into ¼-inch-thick slices

¾-pound mozzarella, cut into ¼-inch-thick slices

8 leaves basil, finely sliced, or 2 tablespoons dried oregano

1 Prepare the dressing, whisking together the vinegar and salt and pepper in a small mixing bowl. Slowly whisk in the oil until the dressing is smooth. Set aside.

2 Line 4 plates with the arugula leaves. Arrange alternating slices of tomato and mozzarella over the arugula to form a circle.

3 Sprinkle the salad with basil and drizzle with the prepared dressing. Serve immediately after the salad is dressed.

The real mozzarella di bufala

A lot of restaurants make a big deal about their mozzarella. Menus shout about cheese that comes from Italy. And this mozzarella certainly was never shrink-wrapped. The original mozzarella was made in the countryside of Campania and Latium from water buffaloes, a cousin to the American bison. In those regions, cheese is still sometimes made from water buffalo's milk rather than cow's milk, hence the name mozzarella di bufala. This cheese is prized for its intense flavor, porcelain white color, and compact but moist texture. Don't cook with this cheese. Heat destroys all the subtleties that cost so much money. It's shown to its best advantage when served fresh in salads, such as Tomato and Mozzarella Salad, Capri Style.

This highly perishable cheese is sometimes shipped by air. However, it's not a very good traveler. After a few days, the delicate, sweet flavor and creamy texture are lost. If you have a good Italian market or cheese shop that imports mozzarella di bufala, ask when their shipment arrived before buying. If the answer is last week, stick with fresh mozzarella made closer to home.

Leafy Salads

In Italy, leafy salads are served after dinner and before dessert. This may be one reason why bitter greens, such as arugula and radicchio, are so popular. The assertive flavor of the salad cleanses the palate and acts as a transition between the main course and dessert.

You can also serve bold greens American style, before dinner. Their strong flavors stimulate the appetite, and you don't need to consume tremendous quantities to quell hunger pangs. Can you say that about iceberg lettuce with store-bought dressing?

Don't drown greens with too much dressing. Add just enough dressing to coat the greens. They should glisten with just the lightest sheen of oil and vinegar. Never add so much dressing that the leaves become soggy. Tastes vary, but we generally use ¼ cup of dressing per 8 cups of salad greens—enough salad for four servings.

For the dressing to cling to greens, they must be perfectly dry. Oil and vinegar will slide off wet lettuce leaves and pool up at the bottom of the salad bowl. Yuck! A salad spinner does a good job of drying greens, but it doesn't hurt to then pat greens with paper towels to remove all traces of moisture.

Gosh, those greens are bitter

Italians find the bitter bite of peppery arugula or sharp radicchio refreshing. But fill a bowl with too much arugula, radicchio, and endive, and eating salad can become a test of machismo.

If you are not so wild about bitter greens, we know of several ways to keep the punch under control:

- **Mix bitter greens (such as arugula, radicchio, endive, and chicory) with milder greens (such as leaf lettuces).** Salads will have some bite, but they won't be so assertive that kids will run from the table.

- **Dress bitter greens with a dressing that is low in acidity.** A sharp, acidic dressing makes the greens taste even more bitter. Try using lemon juice in place of vinegar (it has half the acidity), or make sure to use a high ratio of oil-to-vinegar in your dressing, at least 4 parts oil to 1 part vinegar.

Hearty Salads

Many Italian salads don't contain a single leafy green. In other cases, the greens are merely a bed for the "main" ingredients. Italians enjoy all kinds of room-temperature foods, including vegetable, seafood, or chicken salads bound with dressing. For most of these recipes, the main ingredient is cooked, dressed, and then cooled to room temperature.

Leafy salads are light and refreshing, but composed salads are generally more substantial and are designed to make a light meal or lunch, especially if they contain meat or seafood. (No, you don't need a music degree, but often you do need to assemble or compose the elements in these recipes on a plate rather than tossing them in a salad bowl.) Composed salads are especially appealing during warm weather—that's why they're popular in Italy. You can also served a composed salad as an antipasto.

Tuscan Bread Salad

Italians cooks are thrifty by nature. They find uses for everything, including stale bread, which gets used in delicious summer salads. Bread that is too fresh makes the salad soggy, and bread that is too hard doesn't soften up enough. To take the guesswork out of this dish, we suggest toasting slices of fresh Italian bread in a 300° oven until dry but not brown, about 5 to 7 minutes. If you have some stale bread on hand, you can use it instead, but be prepared to adjust the marinating time to achieve the right texture. You can add canned tuna and/or anchovies to make this salad more substantial.

Italian recipe name: *Panzanella*

Preparation time: *20 minutes*

Cooking time: *None (1 hour marination)*

Yield: *4 to 6 servings*

6 slices Italian bread, toasted and cut into ½-inch cubes

4 ripe tomatoes, cut into 1-inch cubes

2 stalks celery, cut crosswise into ½-inch pieces

1 medium onion, peeled and thinly sliced

1 small cucumber, skinned, seeded, halved lengthwise, and cut into ⅛-inch crescents

¾ cup olive oil

½ cup red wine vinegar

1 cup fresh basil, sliced into long ribbons

Salt and pepper to taste

Combine all ingredients in a large bowl, toss, and let sit for 1 hour.

Serve at room temperature.

Lentil Salad

In Umbria, the farmers grow especially small and flavorful lentils. Unfortunately, these lentils are not exported. You can use regular supermarket brown lentils in this recipe, but if you make it with green lentils from France, called lentils du Puy, the results are especially good. These tiny green lentils hold their shape well and are excellent in salads like this one.

Italian recipe name: *Insalata di Lenticchie*

Preparation time: *15 minutes*

Cooking time: *None (30 minutes marination)*

Yield: *4 to 6 servings*

2½ cups cooked lentils

1 medium onion, peeled and chopped

2 shallots, finely chopped

1 tomato, chopped

2 tablespoons chopped parsley

½ cup olive oil

¼ cup wine vinegar

Salt and pepper to taste

1 Combine all ingredients in a small bowl.

2 Allow flavors to combine for at least 30 minutes before serving. Serve at room temperature.

Chapter 5

• • • • • • • • • •

Soup's On

In This Chapter

• • • • • • • • • • • • • • • • • •

▶ Making soup, Italian Style

▶ Using stock versus water

▶ Making soup a meal with pasta, rice, beans, and bread

• • • • • • • • • • • • • • • • • •

Few dishes capture the essence of Italian cuisine like a bowl of hot soup. Soup in Italy is a humble dish, with its roots in *la cucina povera,* or the cooking of the poor. In not-too-distant times, soup was considered a meal. Historically, Italian cooks would cobble together nourishing, tasty suppers out of a few vegetables and maybe some beans or stale bread. These soups are generally thick, and never pureed. Rich cream soups are a rarity in Italy, at least in traditional home cooking.

Zuppa (zoop-pa) is the Italian word for soup. If you eat in Italian restaurants, you may recognize the term *zuppa di pesce*. With several kinds of seafood, this soup bespeaks of abundance. However, most Italian soups prepared at home are much simpler and less costly to make. For example, Pappa al Pomodoro, a traditional summer soup from Tuscany, is nothing more than ripe tomatoes simmered with water, basil, garlic, and olive oil and then thickened with leftover bread to create a thick, paplike texture (like baby food). Despite these humble ingredients, Pappa al Pomodoro is one of the most beloved dishes in Tuscany.

This chapter focuses on simple recipes that rely on beans, pasta, bread, and vegetables to create hearty, delicious soups that reveal the artistry and magic of Italian home cooking.

Making Soup—The Basics

Making soup requires very little equipment and allows for plenty of latitude in the kitchen. You can often use vegetables, herbs, and beans interchangeably. If spinach is unavailable, you can use chard or kale (or even arugula) instead. Likewise, you can enrich a soup thickened and made hearty with pasta with rice instead. Soup-making is ideal for the cook who prefers not to follow rules.

That said, you need to know general procedures and have certain pieces of equipment. Soup requires a pot of some sort. A pot with a heavy bottom is preferable because many recipes call for sautéing onions and other vegetables in fat before adding the liquid ingredients. If you make soup in small batches, a 4- or 5-quart pot will suffice. For larger batches, a 6- to 8-quart pot will be better.

When choosing a pot size, make sure that the ingredients will not come too close to the top. Nothing is worse than a boil-over that spills precious soup onto the range top. In many recipes, you will need a pot with a cover. The cover allows the cook to control the rate at which the liquid evaporates. When soup is cooked uncovered, much of the stock or water evaporates, and the result is a thick soup. Of course, if you want something more brothy, you can opt to leave the cover on.

Whether the cover is on or off, keep the liquid at a modest simmer. In most recipes, we recommend that you heat the liquid until it reaches a boil and then reduce the temperature to a simmer. (When the surface is covered with large popping bubbles, the soup is at a boil. When the soup is at simmer, small bubbles should rise gently to the surface.) Simmering, rather than boiling, ensures that vegetables, beans, and other ingredients soften without disintegrating.

In most recipes, we suggest that you season throughout the cooking process. When making soups, you need to be careful, though, not to add too much salt at the start. This is especially important in soups that are cooked uncovered. As the liquid reduces, what tastes like the right amount of salt becomes more concentrated in the remaining liquid, and the soup may be too salty by the time it's ready to be served. Go lightly at the start with the salt and then adjust the seasoning after the soup has cooked down sufficiently.

When soup is ready, it's time to dig out a ladle from the drawer; it's so much quicker and neater than using a spoon or pouring the soup straight from the pot. If you like your soup especially hot, use ovenproof ceramic soup bowls and warm them in a 200° oven for 10 minutes. (The bowls will be hot, so use oven mitts to handle them and warn diners that the bowls are hot.) The heat from the bowls will keep the soup piping hot, right to the last spoonful.

Most soups work well as leftovers, reheated the next day. Soups with pasta, rice, and bread are the exceptions. These ingredients become mushy if reheated. Although these soups taste fine, the texture is not as appealing as when freshly made. In general, you can keep soups in the refrigerator for up to two days. If you want to store soup longer, place it in airtight containers and pop the containers in the freezer. Make sure to leave some headroom at the top of the containers because the soup will expand slightly as it freezes. Soup can be kept in the freezer for several months. Defrost frozen soup in the refrigerator before reheating.

Soup should be reheated over medium-low heat and stirred often to prevent the bottom from scorching. Sometimes the texture of the soup seems quite thick when it's being reheated. Thin the soup with water or stock until the desired consistency is achieved and adjust the seasoning if needed.

Making Stock

Many Italian soups use water as their base, while others start with meat, chicken, fish, or vegetable stock. Stock is made by simmering bones, scraps of meat, parts with little use (like chicken backs or fish heads), and/or chopped vegetables and herbs in water. The solids flavor the water to create a rich base, called stock, that can be used to make soups or sauces.

Some cooks are under the misconception that the stock pot is the place to use limp vegetables, old scraps of meat, and other kitchen leftovers. However, stock tastes only as good as the ingredients used to make it. Meat should be fresh and trimmed of as much fat and gristle as possible. Vegetables should be fresh and clean. Although stock is the perfect place to use up a stray onion or carrot, don't add anything to the stock pot that you would not consider fresh enough to eat.

You can control the intensity of the stock in several ways. At the outset, you can change the ratio of solids to liquid. In general, you want to add enough water to cover the solid ingredients by an inch or two. Add more water, and the resulting stock will be weak, which may be fine for risotto but is not appropriate for brothy soup that needs a potent stock. If the solids are just barely covered with water, the stock will be more intense in flavor.

After the solids and water are in the pot, bring everything to a boil and then reduce the heat to a gentle simmer. As the solids cook, they may throw off some impurities in the form of foam, which should be skimmed off with a spoon and discarded.

After the solid ingredients have given up their flavor, the contents of the stock pot are poured through a mesh strainer set over a clean container or pot. (This flavor-finding mission happens quickly—in less than an hour—for vegetables and fish; for chicken and meat, this process can take two or three hours.) The strainer traps the solids. To release as much flavor as possible from the solids, press down on them with the back of a large spoon to squeeze out their juices. A French strainer, called a chinois, has a conical shape that makes it especially easy to extract every last bit of flavor from the stock ingredients.

To intensify the flavor of a finished stock, place the strained liquid back over the heat and cook until reduced to the desired consistency. Because stock is often reduced, salt is generally not added until the stock is ready to be used. When the stock is done, it should be cooled until the fat congeals on top. This fat can be removed with a spoon or skimmer and discarded.

Defatted stock should be placed in an airtight container and refrigerated for up to three days or frozen for up to several months. When freezing stock, divide a single batch into several smaller containers so that you can pull out just as much as you need when making recipes in the future. Or, freeze stock in ice cube trays and store the frozen cubes in plastic bags.

Stock portfolio

Cooks who want to plan strategically for the future should keep chicken, fish, and vegetable stock in the freezer.

✔ **Chicken stock:** Chicken stock is by far the most versatile stock. It's rarely inappropriate (beef stock in fish soup is odd, but chicken stock will taste just fine) and is often the best choice. Use backs, necks, wings, or even drumsticks to make stock. In most cases, the chicken should be balanced with a handful or two of chopped vegetables (onion, carrot, and celery are the usual choices) and perhaps 1 or 2 bay leaves, several peeled garlic cloves, and a dozen or so whole black peppercorns. You can also add some whole parsley sprigs. The chicken is essential; the vegetables are nice but optional.

To make about 2 quarts chicken stock, start with 3 pounds chicken parts (remove any fat and skin first) in a pot and cover with 2½ quarts water. Add vegetables and herbs and simmer for at least 2 hours to extract the full flavor from the chicken.

✔ **Fish stock:** Fish stock has limited uses (for chowders, other fish soups, and seafood risotto), but it can make a good dish great, adding depth of flavor and intensity. Fish stock is usually made from scraps such as heads, bones, and tails from fish, as well as shells from lobster or shrimp. Avoid oily fish, such as salmon, which makes the stock too fishy. Fish with mild, white, flaky flesh, such as red snapper or flounder, are best for stock. Make sure that innards and gills don't go into the stock pot because they impart an off flavor.

To make about 2 quarts fish stock, place 2 pounds fish heads, bones, tails, and fins in a pot and cover with 2 quarts water. Add aromatics like bay leaves, parsley, and thyme sprigs, and whole black peppercorns and simmer for about 30 minutes to extract the flavor from the fish. (Do not cook too long, or the stock will become too fishy.) Many chefs use a little wine along with water as the liquid. The acidity from the wine balances the fish flavor nicely. If you want to use white wine, add 1 cup for every 2 quarts water. You can add a halved lemon as well.

✔ **Vegetable stock:** Some chefs argue that light vegetable dishes, such as an asparagus risotto, are overwhelmed by rich chicken stock and that a milder vegetable stock is the better route. Other chefs find vegetable stocks insipid and prefer to use chicken stock in most every application, other than seafood soups. One camp appreciates the mild sweetness of good vegetable stock, while the other camp wishes vegetable stock were richer and stronger tasting, like chicken stock.

We tend to agree that vegetable stock is nice in certain applications where chicken stock can overwhelm the flavor of vegetables. However, you must use good vegetable stock. Throwing a chicken into a pot with some water produces good stock. Add some aromatic vegetables such as onions and carrots, and you have great stock. Vegetable stock requires more thought and more work.

To coax flavor from the vegetables, we recommend that you sauté them in a little olive oil before adding the water. Using lots of vegetables (at least a cup of chopped vegetables for every cup of water) is imperative. Leeks, onions, carrots, and celery are a must. Typical seasonings include fresh herbs (especially thyme, basil, and parsley sprigs), dried bay leaves, and whole black peppercorns. Add potatoes to give the stock some body, peeled garlic cloves for some intensity, a little dried porcini for some earthy flavor and color, and a chopped tomato or two for color. Finely chop all vegetables so that they release as much flavor as possible.

To make about 2 quarts vegetable stock, place 10 cups finely chopped vegetables in a pot along with 2 tablespoons olive oil. Sauté until the vegetables are golden, 10 to 12 minutes. Add 10 cups water and then simmer until the vegetables have given up their flavor, about 1 hour. When straining the stock, press firmly on the vegetables to extract all their juices.

Chicken Soup with Pasta and Eggs

At its simplest, stracciatella is just eggs cooked in chicken stock. It's not all that different from the egg drop soup served at your local Chinese restaurant. In fact, this soup will even look like Chinese egg drop soup—with egg "rags" obvious. We like to add a little orzo, a tiny pasta shaped like rice, or broken spaghetti, but the pasta isn't essential. This recipe is typical of the cooking from the Jewish ghetto in Rome. High-quality homemade chicken stock really makes a difference in a such a simple dish. Some Roman recipes for stracciatella add the juice of half a lemon to the egg mixture. The acidity helps balance some of the richness from the chicken stock, eggs, and cheese.

Italian recipe name: *Stracciatella*

Preparation time: *5 minutes*

Cooking time: *10 minutes*

Yield: *4 servings*

4 cups homemade chicken stock or canned chicken broth, divided

¼ cup orzo or spaghetti, broken into 1-inch pieces

2 eggs

3 tablespoons grated Parmigiano-Reggiano

Salt and pepper to taste

1 tablespoon chopped fresh chives

1 Transfer ¼ cup stock to a small bowl. Set aside. Pour the remaining stock into a medium saucepan and bring to a boil. Add the pasta and reduce the heat so that it gently boils.

2 Add the eggs, Parmigiano-Reggiano, and salt and pepper to the reserved stock. Beat with a whisk for about 2 minutes. Slowly add the egg mixture to the simmering stock and pasta, stirring constantly. Continue to simmer for 8 minutes. Season with salt and pepper.

3 Before serving, add the chives. Top with additional grated cheese, if desired.

Using Water Rather than Stock

Many Italian peasant soups call for water. These recipes originated in times or places when meat was scarce. Because you don't need to make any stock, these recipes are appealing to modern cooks. Over the years, Italian cooks have found ways to make these simple soups rich in flavor.

What about canned broth?

Stock requires some planning, and you may not always have some on hand. Clearly, this happens very often, and that's why canned broths and bouillon cubes are so popular. (We don't know why, but when you cook chicken in water yourself, this resulting liquid is called stock. If you buy the same thing in a can, it's called broth.)

Italians are more likely to use a bouillon cube (called a *dado* in Italian) than canned broth. In the United States, we find that the bouillon cubes have an off-taste, and we generally

avoid them. Canned broths, especially those that are low in sodium, are decent, if not great.

The flavor of chicken seems to translate best in canned broth. Canned beef broths have little meat flavor, and canned vegetable stocks are usually overly sweet. Remember you can always use water in an Italian soup if you have any doubts about the quality of canned broth. For more information, see the "Using Water Rather than Stock" section. (No one makes canned fish broth. Bottled clam juice is the usual substitute.)

First and foremost, start with cold, clean water. Hot water may seem like a timesaver, but it often picks up a metallic flavor in the water heater and should not be used when cooking soup or anything else, including tea or pasta. Also, make sure that all the ingredients that go into a water-based soup are extremely fresh and flavorful. Good chicken stock can compensate for lackluster vegetables better than plain water.

Besides using good ingredients, many Italian cooks rely on a number of flavor boosters when making water-based soups:

✔ Save the rinds from Parmigiano-Reggiano (they can be kept in the freezer in a zipper-lock bag for months) and add one rind to a pot of minestrone or other soup that can be served with grated cheese. The rind softens, but doesn't fall apart, as the soup cooks. When you're ready to serve the soup, just remember to fish out the rind and discard it. The cheese rind gives soups a rich buttery, nutty flavor.

- ✔ Soak some dried porcini mushrooms in hot water for 20 minutes, or until soft. Add the mushrooms and the strained soaking liquid to any soup that calls for mushrooms, and you'll get a heartier, fuller flavor.

- ✔ Sauté pancetta along with some vegetables in a little olive oil to heighten the flavor of the soup. The pancetta adds a salty, subtle pork flavor that is welcome in most soups.

- ✔ Swirl pesto or another herb paste (you can use something as simple as chopped fresh rosemary and minced garlic bound with olive oil) directly into the soup pot after the heat has been turned off. Even better, dollop a little pesto into each soup bowl just before serving. The heat releases the flavor of the basil and garlic, stimulating the olfactory senses as well as the taste buds.

- ✔ Grate some fresh cheese, especially Parmigiano-Reggiano or Pecorino Romano, directly into individual soup bowls.

- ✔ Drizzle high-quality extra-virgin olive oil into soup bowls at the table. Again, the heat of the soup releases the aroma from the oil and heightens the flavor of the soup.

Creating Hearty Soups with Pasta, Rice, Beans, and Bread

Many Italian soups are made especially hearty by adding pasta, rice, beans, or bread to the pot. The texture becomes thick—almost stewlike—and these soups, which are usually vegetable-based, become a complete meal. You can add a salad or vegetable side dish, but otherwise these soups are one-dish meals.

Pasta and rice in the pot

Pasta is almost always added when the soup is nearly done. The pasta should still be a bit al dente, not mushy or falling apart, when the soup is served. Tiny pasta shapes may need as little as 5 or 10 minutes of cooking; thicker shapes may need to simmer for 15 minutes. The soup should be fairly brothy when the pasta is added. If the soup has cooked down, add a little water or stock, and return the liquid to a boil before adding the pasta.

Rice is treated in the same fashion as pasta. It should be cooked in the soup pot for as long as it takes to soften the grains. In general, 20 minutes is enough time. Regular long-grain rice is fine, but if you have some arborio rice on hand, use it in soups. The grains will remain slightly chewy and are less likely to fall apart.

Both pasta and rice thicken soups by absorbing excess liquid as they soften and by throwing off some starch that gives body to the remaining liquid. As the pasta and rice cook, add more water if the soup is becoming too thick.

Beans in the pot

Dried beans can be cooked right in the soup. The starch that the beans give off as they soften gives the soup body. If cooked long enough, the beans fall apart and make an especially thick, almost creamy, soup.

You can cook dried beans separately and then add them to the soup pot about five minutes before serving, simply to heat them through. You can also use canned beans, which have been drained and rinsed, in this kind of recipe.

Pasta and Bean Soup

If pressed for time, place all the ingredients for the soup in the pot—except the pasta—and simmer until tender. Cook the pasta in the soup until al dente and serve. Whether making the quick or regular version of this recipe, you can sprinkle each serving of the soup with 1 tablespoon grated Parmigiano-Reggiano cheese.

Italian recipe name: *Pasta e Fagioli*

Preparation time: *20 minutes (plus overnight soaking for dried beans)*

Cooking time: *2 hours*

Yield: *6 to 8 servings*

Special tool: *Food processor*

½ cup dried cranberry beans

½ cup dried kidney beans

½ cup dried pinto beans
2 medium potatoes, peeled and diced

5 cloves garlic (3 cloves peeled and crushed; 2 cloves peeled and minced)

1 sprig fresh rosemary plus 1 tablespoon chopped fresh rosemary

1 sprig fresh sage plus 2 teaspoons chopped fresh sage

4 quarts cold water

1 tablespoon salt

½ cup olive oil, divided

4 ounces (about 8 slices) pancetta or bacon

1 small onion, peeled and chopped

1 leek, white part only, thoroughly rinsed and chopped

1 small celery stalk, chopped

1 medium carrot, chopped

¼ teaspoon hot red pepper flakes

½ cup white wine

6 tablespoons tomato paste

½ pound dry short-cut pasta, such as pennette

Salt and pepper to taste

1 Rinse the beans, picking through them to remove any pebbles. Soak the beans overnight in a medium bowl with 5 cups cold water. Drain.

2 Put the beans in a large soup pot with the potatoes, crushed garlic, rosemary sprig, and sage sprig. Add the water and bring the mixture to a boil. Add the salt and reduce the heat to a low boil. Cook, covered, until the beans are soft enough to crush easily between 2 fingers, about 40 to 45 minutes.

3 Transfer half of the bean mixture to the bowl of a food processor. Puree until smooth. Return the bean puree to the soup pot.

4 Heat ¼ cup olive oil in a medium skillet. Add the pancetta, minced garlic, chopped rosemary, chopped sage, onion, leek, celery, carrot, and red pepper flakes. Cook over medium heat, stirring occasionally, until the onion is soft and the mixture just starts to brown, about 12 to 15 minutes.

5 Add the wine to the vegetables and cook until the liquid is completely absorbed, about 2 to 3 minutes.

6 Transfer the contents of the skillet to the soup pot with the beans. Add the tomato paste. Stir to combine. Bring the soup mixture to a boil and then reduce the heat to maintain a low boil. Cook for 40 minutes, stirring occasionally.

7 Add the pasta to the soup. Cook for another 8 to 12 minutes (depending on the cooking time of the pasta; check package instructions). Adjust the consistency of the soup as desired, adding up to 2 more cups of water. Adjust seasoning with salt and pepper. Serve soup hot, drizzled with remaining ¼ cup olive oil.

Lentil Soup

Unlike other dried legumes, lentils are never soaked and are always cooked in the soup pot with the other ingredients. Lentil soup is a traditional dish for an Italian New Year's Eve celebration. Lentils are thought to bring good luck and money in the new year.

Italian recipe name: *Zuppa di Lenticchie*

Preparation time: *20 minutes*

Cooking time: *40 to 45 minutes*

Yield: *8 servings*

2 tablespoons olive oil

1 medium onion, peeled and chopped

1 medium carrot, peeled and chopped

2 celery stalks, chopped

4 cloves garlic, peeled and chopped

4 sprigs fresh sage, chopped, or 1 teaspoon dried sage

2 cups white wine

16-ounce can chopped Italian plum tomatoes, drained

1½ cups or 10 ounces dried green or brown lentils

2 medium potatoes, peeled and cut into 1-inch chunks

4 slices of pancetta (optional)

2 quarts cold water

Salt and pepper to taste

1 Heat the olive oil in a large saucepan. Add the onion, carrot, celery, garlic, and sage and cook over medium heat, stirring frequently, until the onion is translucent, about 7 minutes.

2 Add the wine and cook until it reduces or evaporates completely.

3 Add the tomatoes and cook for 5 more minutes and then add the lentils, potatoes, pancetta (if using), and water. Bring the mixture to a boil, reduce the heat, and simmer for 20 minutes. Test the lentils to see whether they're cooked; they should be tender but still have a slightly firm bite.

4 Season the soup with salt and pepper. If a slightly creamy texture is desired, puree half of the soup in a food processor, return the puree to the saucepan, and simmer for another 5 minutes, stirring frequently.

Bread in soup

Everyone knows that bread makes a great accompaniment to a bowl of soup. Italians take this logic one step further and actually add bread to the soup as it cooks. Stale cubes or slices soften in the pot and give soup heft and texture. Some cooks prefer to let the bread swell but still retain its shape. Others like the bread to fall apart. Depending on the size of the pieces and how stale they are, bread cubes require 5 to 10 minutes of cooking to soften and 30 to 40 minutes to fall apart.

As with pasta and rice, bread absorbs liquid and makes soups very thick. Make sure that the soup is still brothy when adding bread and thin out the texture before serving, if desired.

Most recipes calling for bread rely on country white bread. You can use a baguette or sourdough bread. However, avoid breads with seeds or nuts, which will float free in the soup.

Tuscan Bread and Tomato Soup

This classic summertime soup is made in Tuscany with fresh ripe tomatoes. In the winter, Tuscans make a similar soup called *pancotto,* or "cooked bread," which is brothier and contains a little tomato paste or canned tomatoes. However, Pappa al Pomodoro is about the tomatoes, so use the sweetest, ripest tomatoes you can find. The bread cubes in this recipe are cooked for a fairly long time and will fall apart to create a thick, porridgelike consistency, hence the name for the soup, which translates as "tomato pap."

Italian recipe name: *Pappa al Pomodoro*

Preparation time: *15 minutes*

Cooking time: *1 hour*

Yield: *4 servings*

½ cup olive oil, divided

1 leek, white part only, thoroughly rinsed and chopped

1 small red onion, peeled and chopped

6 cloves garlic, peeled and chopped

½ cup white wine

½ cup chopped fresh basil, divided, or 1 tablespoon dried basil and 1 teaspoon dried oregano

1½ pounds ripe tomatoes (about 5 medium), peeled, seeded, and chopped, or one 20-ounce can of plum tomatoes

2 cups cold water

1½ cups cubed bread (1-day-old Italian country, or semolina bread)

Salt and pepper to taste

½ cup grated Parmigiano-Reggiano

1 In a large saucepan, heat ¼ cup olive oil over medium heat. Add the leek, onion, and garlic and cook until the vegetables just start to brown, about 5 minutes. Do not allow the garlic to burn.

2 Add the wine and maintain a low boil until it reduces to about 1 tablespoon of liquid, 5 to 8 minutes.

3 Add ¼ cup basil, the tomatoes, and water. Bring the mixture to a boil, reduce the heat, and simmer uncovered for 15 minutes. Add the bread. Cook, stirring occasionally, for another 20 minutes.

4 Season the soup with salt and pepper, add the remaining ¼ cup basil, and cook for 10 more minutes.

5 Serve hot drizzled with the remaining ¼ cup olive oil. Sprinkle with the Parmigiano-Reggiano cheese.

Chapter 6

• • • • • • • • • •

Fresh Pasta

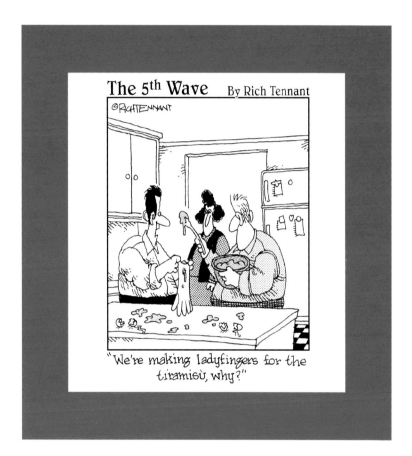

The 5th Wave   By Rich Tennant

"We're making ladyfingers for the tiramisù, why?"

Fresh pasta is a project, but, oh, what fun. If you liked working with Play-Doh as a kid, you'll enjoy turning flour and eggs into thin ribbons of dough for fettuccine or see-through sheets for lasagne. But be warned: Don't plan on serving fresh pasta on a weeknight after a long day at work or taking care of your kids—at least, not if you want to make the pasta yourself.

Most Italian towns, no matter how small, have a shop, called a *pastificio,* that makes fresh fettuccine, tagliorini, ravioli, and agnolotti. These pastas are prepared every day and sold fresh. If you want to make the recipes in this chapter but don't have the time to make your own fresh pasta, go to a gourmet store or pasta shop that makes its own pasta every day.

But whatever you do, please, please, don't buy the so-called "fresh" pasta sold in the refrigerated case at the supermarket. This pasta is expensive and cooks up mushy and tasteless. Fresh pasta was never meant to sit for weeks in the supermarket. It may be edible for weeks or months (at least according to the sell-by dates stamped on most packages), but it's not fresh in the truest sense of the word. Fresh pasta loses its flavor and delicate texture very quickly, so either make it yourself or buy it from someone who makes it fresh every day, like people do in Italy.

Making Pasta Yourself

Traditionally, certain dishes require fresh pasta. For example, filled pastas, such as ravioli, must start with fresh pasta. For other dishes, such as lasagne, you have a choice of fresh or dried pasta.

Although dried lasagne noodles and fettuccine exist, the fresh versions are far superior. Fresh noodles actually absorb some of the creamy sauces that are usually served with these pasta shapes. In contrast, butter, cheese, and cream sauces slide right off dried pasta. The delicate egg flavor of fresh pasta also complements these kinds of delicate, creamy sauces. If you want to make the dishes we discuss in this chapter, we really urge you to use fresh pasta.

Making pasta at home was once a challenge. The dough had to be kneaded by hand and then rolled out with much finesse into thin sheets that you then cut into the appropriate shape. You can still make pasta this way, but two modern inventions (the food processor and pasta machine) have made fresh pasta much more accessible, even for novices. Here's what you need to know.

Choosing the ingredients

Fresh pasta requires only four ingredients—flour, eggs, olive oil, and salt. Flour produces fresh noodles that are delicate yet elastic enough to stretch and roll out. Unbleached flour is the closest thing to the flour used to make fresh pasta in Italy, although bleached flour, which has been treated with chemicals to make it whiter, also works.

The other main ingredient is eggs. Use the freshest eggs possible because they provide pasta with most of its flavor. And a tiny bit of olive oil can be used to make the dough more supple and flavorful. A pinch of salt adds flavor as well. The flour and eggs are essential, but you can consider the oil and salt optional but recommended.

You can flavor egg pasta in numerous ways. (For more information, see the sidebar "Flavoring egg pasta.") However, many of these flavorings are for cosmetic rather than flavor reasons. For example, tomato paste can dye fresh egg pasta a beautiful orange-red color. But close your eyes, and you won't be able to taste the difference between plain and tomato pasta.

Some flavorings do provide subtle flavors that you can detect if the sauce is especially delicate. (For example, a plain cream sauce shows off the flavor of saffron or black pepper pasta.) However, after you put a spicy tomato sauce on any flavored pasta, you taste the sauce, not the pasta. Flavor fresh pasta if you like, but realize that flavoring is mostly an aesthetic decision.

Flavoring egg pasta

You can add two types of flavoring agents to pasta dough. Relatively dry ingredients, such as flour, spices, and herbs, are easy to work with because they don't affect the ratio of flour to eggs.

However, after you add something moist, such as cooked spinach, the dough becomes stickier and harder to work with. You can add more flour, but we suggest avoiding this problem by making sure that all moist additions to pasta dough are as dry as possible. This means adding tomato paste, not fresh tomatoes, to pasta dough or squeezing every last bit of water out of cooked spinach leaves.

We have listed the following flavorings in order of ease. (By the way, you can make chocolate pasta, but it's not Italian. We have chosen traditional flavorings.) Start with things like herbs and black pepper because they don't make the dough harder to work with. After you feel like you have mastered the art of making fresh pasta, try spinach or tomatoes.

You can add all the following ingredients to the recipe for Fresh Egg Pasta, later in this chapter. Add dry ingredients along with the flour; add wet ingredients to the food processor along with the last egg.

✔ **Black pepper:** Coarsely ground black pepper gives egg pasta a mild spiciness and speckled appearance. Use 1½ teaspoons coarsely ground black pepper.

✔ **Saffron:** Saffron threads dye fresh pasta a brilliant yellow-orange color and give it a mild, earthy flavor. Saffron pasta is especially good with tomato-cream sauces. Use ¼ teaspoon crumbled saffron threads.

✔ **Fresh herbs:** Finely minced herbs add fresh green color as well as subtle flavor to egg pasta. Use 2 tablespoons minced fresh parsley, basil, mint, sage, thyme, oregano, or marjoram.

✔ **Whole wheat flour:** Whole wheat flour produces a hearty pasta suitable for chunky meat and vegetable sauces made with olive oil rather than butter. Because it contains more gluten, whole wheat dough takes a minute or two longer to knead into a smooth ball. Replace 1½ cups flour with an equal amount of whole-wheat flour.

✔ **Buckwheat flour:** Buckwheat pasta is a specialty of the Lombardy region. It's traditionally served with hearty sauces made with leafy greens, cabbage, and potatoes. It has a wholesome, nutty flavor and chewy texture. Buckwheat flour isn't actually made from grain; it's made from the seed of a plant in the rhubarb family. Replace ½ cup flour with an equal amount of buckwheat flour.

✔ **Tomatoes:** Tomato paste dyes fresh pasta a pale orange color but adds little or no flavor. Use 2 tablespoons tomato paste and be prepared to add an extra ¼ cup flour to keep the dough from becoming too sticky.

✔ **Spinach:** Spinach adds no flavor but gives a good color to fresh pasta. Spinach noodles are appropriate in most recipes that call for fresh pasta. Because flavor is not an issue, start with frozen chopped spinach. Put half of a 10-ounce package in some boiling water and cook 2 to 3 minutes until tender. Drain the spinach in a colander, pressing on it with the back of a large spoon to remove as much water as possible. Place the spinach on a cutting board and finely chop it. Press the spinach with your hands, tilting the board over the sink to drain off any remaining liquid. You should have about ⅓ cup finely chopped spinach. Squeezing out all the liquid you can is imperative, or the dough becomes sticky.

Making the dough

Before the invention of the food processor, making the dough for fresh pasta took about 20 minutes. With the food processor, it takes about 1 minute. For history buffs, here's how to make it the old-fashioned way.

1. Place the flour in a pile on the counter.

2. Hollow out the center of the pile so that the flour is shaped into a ring.

It looks like the top of a volcano.

3. Crack the eggs and place them in the center of the ring. Add the oil and salt to the eggs.

4. With a fork, slowly incorporate some of the flour into the eggs.

Don't break through the wall of flour and let the eggs run all over the counter!

5. When you've worked enough flour into the eggs so that they won't run away, start kneading to work in the rest of the flour and then to knead the dough.

Pasta dough must be very smooth and well kneaded, so work the dough by hand for at least 10 minutes. When the dough is as smooth as a baby's bottom, you are ready to roll.

The modern method, of course, is just place the flour in a food processor, turn on the machine, add the eggs, and wait about ten seconds. You should still knead the dough by hand after it comes together in the food processor.

Rolling and cutting the dough

After you've kneaded the pasta dough, it's time to rock and roll. (Well, you can skip the rock part, but you must roll.) Traditionally, Italian home cooks would use a rolling pin or even a wine bottle. However, stretching the dough out this way is very hard. The dough is tough and resists your best efforts. In the end, pasta rolled with a rolling pin is usually too thick.

We prefer using a manual pasta machine. It rolls the pasta to an even thickness, and you can get the sheets of pasta quite thin. This machine also cuts the pasta. Most models can cut the pasta into fettuccine or spaghetti. The wider fettuccine cutters usually work a little better.

In addition to pasta machines that you crank by hand, you can find several electric extruders on the market. Basically, these are a food processor and pasta machine in one. You put the ingredients in the machine and then press a button to knead and then extrude a variety of shapes.

Unfortunately, most electric pasta machines don't work all that well, and we don't think that they're worth the $200 or so that most companies charge. For that money, you can buy a food processor (for about $150) and a manual pasta machine (for about $40), and the food processor has hundreds of uses. An electric pasta machine is good for only one thing. A manual pasta machine produces two shapes—fettuccine or spaghetti. However, you can take the long sheets of dough and cut them to make lasagne noodles. Or take those long sheets and cut them with a knife into long, wide ribbons to make pappardelle or squares for ravioli or tortellini.

After you have cut out the pasta shape, you need to be careful to keep the individual pieces separated. Letting them dry for a half hour or so helps. You can keep fresh pasta on clean kitchen towels at room temperature for several hours before cooking. For longer storage, place the pasta in a zipper-lock plastic bag and freeze it for up to one month. Don't defrost frozen fresh pasta. Simply take the pasta out of the freezer and dump it into a pot of boiling water. The cooking time is a minute or two longer than for fresh pasta.

Cooking and saucing fresh noodles

Cooking fresh pasta takes less time than you may think. After the water returns to a boil (it takes a minute or two, depending on how much pasta you've added to the pot and how high the heat is), the pasta may be almost done. Start tasting, and just before you think that the pasta is done (it should be cooked through and tender but still have some chew and elasticity), drain it quickly and get it sauced.

Even more so than dried pasta, fresh pasta goes from perfectly cooked to soggy and overcooked very quickly. After the pasta goes into the pot, stay close (no phone calls, please) and taste the pasta often to make sure that you catch it at just the right moment.

Because fresh pasta cooks so quickly, you must finish the sauce before the pasta goes into the pot.

Fresh Egg Pasta

Making your own pasta is surprisingly easy, especially if you use a food processor and manual pasta machine.

Italian recipe name: *Pasta all'Uovo*

Preparation time: *50 minutes*

Cooking time: *None*

Yield: *6 servings*

Special tools: *Food processor, manual pasta machine*

2¼ cups flour plus flour for dusting work surface and pasta

3 eggs

Pinch of salt

½ tablespoon olive oil

1 Place the flour in the bowl of a food processor. With the motor running, add the eggs 1 at a time and then add the salt and olive oil. Process for 10 more seconds.

2 Transfer the dough to a flat, flour-dusted surface. Knead it until it forms a smooth, firm ball, about 5 minutes. Place it in a bowl, cover it with a kitchen towel, and set aside for about 30 minutes.

3 Divide the dough into 5 balls. With the palm of your hand, flatten each ball. Set the wheel for the rollers of the pasta machine on the widest setting. Turning the handle, roll the dough through. Lightly dust the pasta with flour and fold it into thirds. Roll it through the machine again. Repeat this 3 more times, folding the dough each time.

4 Continue rolling the pasta through the machine, dusting it with flour, but no longer folding it in between rolling. Make the opening smaller each time, until you have a long sheet of pasta that is about ¹⁄₁₆-inch thick. It's now ready to be cut into different shapes with the pasta machine.

Lasagne

Make lasagne with dried noodles if you must, but try it with fresh noodles and you really notice the difference. The result is a much lighter, more delicate dish.

In Bologna, lasagne is made with a rich meat sauce. The layers are bound together with a creamy white sauce, called bechamel, and the cheese is Parmigiano-Reggiano. Italians in this region don't use mozzarella or ricotta, which are used primarily in lasagne recipes from southern Italy and the United States.

Bechamel Sauce

You can use this creamy white sauce as a binder in many baked pasta dishes. When making this sauce, you must whisk constantly to prevent the formation of lumps.

Italian recipe name: *Bechamela*

Preparation time: *5 minutes*

Cooking time: *9 minutes*

Yield: *1 quart*

8 tablespoons butter

½ cup flour

1 quart warm milk

Pinch of ground nutmeg

Salt and white pepper to taste

1 In a heavy saucepan, melt the butter. Add the flour and cook, stirring, over low heat for 4 minutes. Increase the heat to medium and gradually add the milk, stirring constantly with a whisk.

2 Continue whisking the sauce as it gently boils, about 5 minutes. Add the nutmeg and salt and pepper. Stir well and remove from heat. Use immediately or store in a bowl with plastic wrap touching the surface of the bechamel so that a skin doesn't form on top. Store, refrigerated, for up to 2 days.

Meat Sauce

This sauce requires very gentle simmering to produce a finely textured, sweet meat sauce that's rich and delicious. You can use the sauce in baked pasta dishes, such as lasagne, or tossed with fresh fettuccine. This sauce stores well, frozen in small containers, for up to 3 weeks.

Italian recipe name: *Ragù di Carne*

Preparation time: *25 minutes*

Cooking time: *3 hours*

Yield: *8 servings*

¼ cup olive oil

1 large onion, peeled and chopped

3 celery stalks, chopped

1 medium carrot, chopped

5 cloves garlic, peeled and minced

¾ pound ground pork

¾ pound ground beef

4 thin slices of pancetta or bacon, minced

4 thin slices of prosciutto, minced

2 cups dry red wine

28-ounce can whole Italian tomatoes, undrained

2 cups water

Salt to taste

½ teaspoon hot red pepper flakes

¼ teaspoon black pepper

Pinch of allspice

Pinch of nutmeg

Pinch of cloves

Pinch of cinnamon

1 In a large pot, heat the olive oil over medium heat. Add the onion, celery, carrot, and garlic and cook, stirring often, until the vegetables are tender, about 15 minutes.

2 Add the pork, beef, pancetta or bacon, and prosciutto and cook, stirring frequently, for another 10 minutes.

3 Add the wine and cook for about 5 minutes. Add the tomatoes and water and simmer, covered, for 50 minutes.

4 Season with the salt, red pepper flakes, black pepper, and spices and then stir. Simmer, stirring occasionally, for 90 more minutes, until the sauce is thick and flavorful. Check the sauce during cooking. If it thickens too quickly, add a little bit of water (about ½ cup at a time) and continue cooking. Adjust seasoning with salt, if necessary.

Lasagne

Lasagne is a lot of work, but you can make the Meat Sauce and Bechamel Sauce in advance. You can assemble the entire lasagne, wrap it tightly in foil, and then refrigerate it for up to 1 day before baking.

Italian recipe name: *Lasagne*

Preparation time: *25 to 30 minutes (excludes time for preparation of Meat Sauce, Bechamel Sauce, and pasta)*

Cooking time: *35 minutes*

Yield: *12 servings*

2 recipes Fresh Egg Pasta

2 tablespoons butter, for greasing the baking dish

1½ recipes Meat Sauce

1 recipe Bechamel Sauce

1 cup grated Parmigiano-Reggiano

1 Preheat oven to 375°.

2 Prepare the pasta. Cut the rolled pasta dough into 8 x 6-inch sheets. Precook the pasta sheets in salted boiling water for 1 minute and then transfer to a large bowl of cold water. After the pasta has cooled, remove the squares and place them on a large platter. Set aside.

3 Butter the bottom and sides of a 9 x 13-inch baking dish. Spread a layer of the meat sauce, about ½ cup, on the bottom of the dish.

4 Line the baking dish with a layer of pasta. Evenly spread a layer of bechamel over the pasta, followed by meat sauce, and then sprinkle with about ¼ cup cheese. Cover with a layer of pasta, bechamel, meat sauce, and cheese. Repeat this process 3 more times. The top layer should have bechamel, meat sauce, and cheese.

5 Bake for 30 to 35 minutes until bubbly and slightly browned on top. Remove from oven, let cool for 10 minutes, and serve.

Filled pastas

You can use fresh pasta to make filled pastas, such as ravioli, agnolotti, and tortellini. Ravioli are the easiest filled pasta to make because they aren't shaped by hand but rather cut into squares.

To make ravioli, you should leave the pasta dough in long sheets. You then dot the filling—spinach and cheese is popular, as is plain cheese—along the length of the pasta sheet. Lay a second sheet over the first and then cut out the ravioli with a scalloped cutter.

If you work quickly, the pasta retains enough moisture to seal on its own. However, as a safety measure, you may want to brush an egg wash over the edges of the pasta sheets to make sure that they stick together. If the edges don't seal properly, the ravioli can open up when boiled. To make an egg wash, beat an egg with a tablespoon or so of water and then use a pastry brush to moisten the edges of the pasta sheets just before you place the second sheet over the filled first sheet.

Spinach Ravioli

You must squeeze all the moisture out of the cooked spinach or the filling becomes watery. Serve these ravioli with the Meat Sauce from the recipe earlier in this chapter or Tomato and Basil Sauce. Or simply serve the ravioli with some melted butter and grated Parmigiano-Reggiano cheese. If you like, warm several minced sage leaves in the melted butter.

Italian recipe name: *Ravioli di Spinaci*

Preparation time: *45 minutes*

Cooking time: *8 minutes*

Yield: *4 servings*

Special tools: *Ravioli cutter, strainer-skimmer*

1 recipe Fresh Egg Pasta

1 cup ricotta

½ cup grated Parmigiano-Reggiano

½ cup cooked spinach, fresh or frozen, water thoroughly squeezed out after cooking

1 egg

1 tablespoon chopped fresh parsley, or 1 teaspoon dried parsley

1 tablespoon chopped fresh thyme

Pinch of ground nutmeg

Pepper to taste

1½ tablespoons salt

Flour for dusting work surface

1 Prepare the pasta. Let it rest, wrapped and refrigerated, for 30 minutes.
To prepare the filling, combine all ingredients (except salt) in a medium bowl. Mix well and set aside.

2 Lay the pasta sheets out on a flat, flour-dusted surface. Place ½ tablespoon dots of the spinach filling, about 3 inches apart, on the bottom layer and fit a second layer of pasta over the first. With your fingers, press down lightly to seal the sheets together and remove any air. Use a scalloped cutter to cut out the ravioli squares.

3 In a large pot, bring 4 quarts water to a boil. Add the salt and half the ravioli. (You should cook the ravioli in 2 batches.) Gently boil for 2 to 4 minutes, until the ravioli rise to the surface. Place the ravioli in a pan, mix with any sauce that you like, and serve.

Chapter 7

• • • • • • • • • •

Poultry: Fowl Fare

The 5th Wave   By Rich Tennant

"Unfortunately, he drives the car like he makes pasta— al dente."

In This Chapter

• • • • • • • • • • • •

▶ Shopping for chicken

▶ Cooking whole birds, parts, and cutlets

▶ Going beyond chicken

• • • • • • • • • • • • • • • •

Chicken has long been popular in Italy. You can't find much open land for raising cattle in Italy, so beef has always been something of a luxury, especially in the country. But anyone with a little backyard can tend chickens, something countless generations of Italians have done. Most old-fashioned Italian chicken recipes begin by sautéing parts in fat and then adding vegetables and liquids, such as tomatoes, wine, or stock, to cook the parts through. This gentle simmering tenderizes tough parts from birds that get a lot of exercise. It also flavors the chicken and creates a rich "sauce" that you can serve over polenta or with mashed potatoes, beans, or bread.

Poultry production has changed remarkably over the past few decades. Mass-produced birds don't get any exercise, and their flesh is rarely tough. Although modern birds may not need the tenderizing effects of braising, the Italian method for cooking chicken still makes sense. Most supermarket chickens are remarkably bland. Cooking them in flavorful liquids helps give them some character.

In addition to explaining how to cook chicken parts in a covered casserole, this chapter also shows you how to turn boneless, skinless chicken cutlets into a number of quick dinners. Chicken cutlets are the ultimate convenience food, adaptable to so many types of preparation.

Fifty years ago, most Italian homes didn't have an oven. Chickens were usually cooked in parts on top of the stove. Therefore, just a few traditional preparations for a whole bird exist. Trussing a chicken is one such preparation. You should do this before adding any seasonings to the outside of the bird. Start by tucking the wings under the bird. Wrap a piece of kitchen twine around the drumsticks. Wrap a second piece of twine around the other end of the bird to hold the wings in place.

Chicken in a Salt Crust

Baking a whole chicken in a salt crust seals in its juices. Truss the chicken before coating the bird with the salt paste. You can carve the chicken in the kitchen as directed in the recipe, but for a more dramatic presentation, bring the chicken right from the oven to the table and open the salt crust before an audience.

Italian recipe name: *Pollo al Sale*

Preparation time: *20 minutes*

Cooking time: *1 hour, 10 minutes*

Yield: *4 servings*

Special tool: *Aluminum foil*

5 cups sea or kosher salt

6 cups flour plus flour for dusting work surface

3 cups water

4 cloves garlic, peeled

1 sprig fresh sage, or 1 teaspoon dried sage

1 sprig fresh rosemary, or 1 teaspoon dried rosemary

3½-pound whole chicken

Salt and pepper to taste

1 Preheat oven to 400°.

2 In a large mixing bowl, combine the sea or kosher salt with flour and water and mix. The mixture should be moist but not wet. Set aside.

3 Place the garlic, sage, and rosemary in the cavity of the chicken. Truss the chicken, tying the legs together. Season with salt and pepper.

4 Line a baking pan with aluminum foil. On a flat flour-dusted surface, roll out the salt dough until it's large enough to completely cover the chicken. Wrap the dough around the chicken and seal tightly. Place the chicken in the baking pan, seam side down.

5 Bake for about 1 hour, 10 minutes. Remove from oven and crack the salt shell with a kitchen mallet or hammer. Lift away the solid pieces of dough. Transfer the chicken to a cutting board and cut into eighths. Transfer portions to each dinner plate and serve.

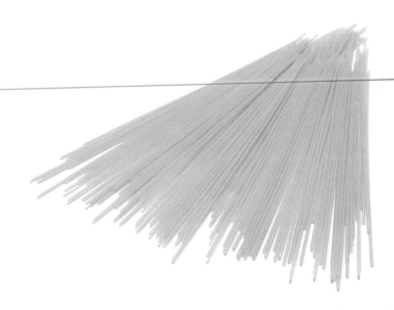

Chicken under a Brick

For this recipe, you remove the backbone from a chicken and then butterfly the chicken. You then grill the butterflied chicken skin side down and weighted so that it cooks evenly. If you don't have any bricks, place a beat-up roasting pan on top of the chicken and then fill the pan with heavy (nonflammable) objects, such as rocks.

This recipe works best with small baby chickens, also called poussins, which you can get from many butcher shops. You can also use large Cornish game hens that weigh about 1½ pounds each. Serve with Sautéed Broccoli Rabe or Stewed Beans with Tomatoes, Sage, and Garlic.

Italian recipe name: *Pollo al Mattone*

Preparation time: *20 minutes (plus 30 minutes for marination)*

Cooking time: *1 hour, 20 minutes*

Yield: *4 servings*

Special tools: *Two bricks, aluminum foil*

2 whole chickens (2 pounds each), cleaned

4 to 6 cloves garlic, peeled and finely sliced

3 tablespoons chopped sage, or 2 teaspoons dried sage

3 tablespoons chopped rosemary, or 2 teaspoons dried rosemary

⅓ cup olive oil

Salt and pepper to taste

Juice of 3 lemons (¾ cup)

2 cups white wine

1 pinch hot red pepper flakes

1 Preheat grill to medium.

2 Butterfly the chickens.

3 In a shallow pan that's just large enough to hold the chickens, combine the garlic, sage, rosemary, and olive oil. Season with salt and pepper and mix. Add the chickens to the pan, turning them over a few times to evenly coat them with the marinade. Leave them covered in the refrigerator for 30 minutes or until you're ready to grill.

4 In a large bowl, combine the lemon juice, wine, and red pepper flakes. Set aside.

5 Wrap 2 bricks in foil. Remove the chickens from their marinade and place them on the grill, skin side down. Place a brick on top of each. Grill for 10 minutes. Turn the chickens, placing the bricks back on top, and grill for another 10 minutes. Remove the bricks. Transfer the chickens to the bowl with the wine mixture, turn to coat the chickens with the mixture, return the chickens to the grill, and place a brick on each chicken. Grill for 10 minutes per side. Repeat this procedure 2 more times, but don't place the bricks on top during the last 10 minutes of cooking. Check the doneness of the chickens by probing the leg meat; the juices should be clear, and the meat shouldn't be at all red or pink.

Baby Chicken with Lemon

In Italy, this dish is made with baby chickens, often called poussins in gourmet stores in the United States and elsewhere. You can also use Cornish game hens from the supermarket in this recipe.

The chickens are cooked in a lot of olive oil to keep them moist. About halfway through the roasting time, the oil is discarded so that the chicken skin can crisp up. Make sure to choose a roasting pan that is deep enough to accommodate all the oil and the chickens.

Italian recipe name: *Polletto al Limone*

Preparation time: *20 minutes*

Cooking time: *50 minutes*

Yield: *4 servings*

4 Cornish game hens or small baby chickens (about 1¼ pounds each)	*2 sprigs fresh rosemary, or 2 teaspoons dried rosemary*
Salt and pepper to taste	*1½ cups olive oil, divided*
1 lemon, quartered	*1 lemon, sliced*
4 cloves garlic, peeled	*Juice of 1 lemon (about 3 tablespoons)*
1 cup white wine	

1 Preheat oven to 375°.

2 Season the hens with salt and pepper outside and inside the cavity. Place 1 lemon quarter, 1 garlic clove, and half a rosemary sprig (or ½ teaspoon dried rosemary) inside each hen. Drizzle the bottom of a roasting pan with ¾ cup oil. Place the hens in the pan and drizzle the remaining ¾ cup oil over the hens.

3 Roast for 10 minutes, turn the hens over, and roast for another 10 minutes. Turn the hens again and cook for another 5 minutes. Drain the fat from the pan and add the lemon slices and lemon juice. Continue cooking for 10 more minutes. Add the wine. Roast until the hens are golden brown, 10 to 15 more minutes. Serve with the pan juices spooned on top.

Take the chicken apart

Most Italian recipes begin with a whole chicken cut into eight parts—two wings, two legs, two thighs, and two breasts. Most Italian cooks do this themselves. You can now buy butchered chicken at almost any supermarket, but here are several good reasons to do this yourself:

- Whole chickens are considerably cheaper than chicken parts.

- Free-range, organic, and kosher chickens are usually sold whole. If you buy chicken parts, they usually come from mass-market birds that have the least flavor.

- When you cut a bird into eight parts, you're left with an extra piece—the back—that you can use to make stock. Just throw the back in a plastic zipper-lock bag in the freezer. When you have several backs, use them to make stock.

Cutting up a whole chicken is easier than it looks. Just put the bird on a cutting board and get out a sharp knife. Follow these steps, and you have the bird ready for cooking in a minute or two:

1. Turn the chicken on its side and pull the wing away from the body.

2. Use the tip of a knife to cut around the joint that attaches the wing to the breast.

Repeat with the second wing.

3. Turn the chicken breast side up.

4. While pulling the leg away from the bird with one hand, use the tip of a knife to slice the skin between the drumstick and breast.

5. With one hand holding the chicken, use the other hand to bend back the thigh and pop out the joint that attaches the leg to the body.

6. Holding the leg away from the body, cut around the joint to release the leg/thigh piece and then detach the other leg/thigh piece.

7. Place the leg/thigh piece skin side down on a cutting board.

8. Use a knife to slice through the fat line and locate the joint; after you locate the joint, cut through to separate the leg and thigh pieces; do this on both sides.

The joint that separates the leg and thigh is underneath a line of fat that divides the thigh and leg.

9. Cut between the bottom of the rib cage and the back of the bird on both sides of the chicken.

When you're finished, the breast and back are completely separated.

Reserve the back for making stock.

10. Starting at the tail end, cut down along one side of the breastbone.

11. When you hit the wishbone, cut down along the side of the wishbone and pop it out of the breast by using your fingers or the tip of the knife.

Repeat on the other side of the breastbone.

Italians often braise or stew chicken parts. In most recipes, the parts are browned and then simmered with a liquid, such as tomatoes, wine, or stock, and vegetables.

Braised Chicken with Mushrooms

Serve with grilled or toasted slices of bread rubbed with garlic and drizzled with a little olive oil.

Italian recipe name: *Cacciucco di Pollo*

Preparation time: *20 minutes*

Cooking time: *1 hour, 20 minutes*

Yield: *4 servings*

3- to 4-pound whole chicken, cut into 8 pieces

Salt and pepper to taste

¼ cup plus 1 tablespoon olive oil

8 cloves garlic, peeled and chopped

2 medium onions, chopped

1 pinch hot red pepper flakes

2 sprigs fresh rosemary, or 1 teaspoon dried rosemary

2 cups white wine

1½ pounds mixed mushrooms (shiitake, oyster, cremini, and/or domestic), quartered or sliced ½-inch thick

3 cups canned plum tomatoes, chopped

2 tablespoons chopped fresh parsley, or 2 teaspoons dried parsley

1 Season the chicken with salt and pepper.

2 Heat the olive oil in a large skillet. Add the garlic, onions, red pepper flakes, and rosemary and sauté, stirring often, for 3 minutes. Then place the chicken pieces in the skillet and cook over medium heat, turning occasionally, for 25 to 30 minutes.

3 Drain the fat from the skillet and add the wine. Simmer to reduce the wine by half. Add the mushrooms, stir, and cook, covered, for 15 minutes. Then add the tomatoes and adjust the seasoning with salt and pepper. Simmer, covered, for 25 minutes, stirring occasionally. Mix in the parsley 3 minutes before serving.

Chicken, the easy way

Boneless, skinless chicken breasts, which are commonly called chicken cutlets, are easy to prepare—just open the package, rinse, and pat dry—and quick to cook. In Italian cooking, they're often used as a cheaper substitute for veal cutlets.

Like you do with veal, you may need to pound chicken cutlets before cooking. Simply place the cutlets between two pieces of plastic wrap and pound with a mallet or the bottom of a heavy pan. Pounding ensures that the chicken cooks evenly, so don't skip this step.

Breaded Chicken Cutlets, Milan Style

For this dish, chicken breasts are coated with bread crumbs and then pan-fried in oil until crisp. This was Cesare's favorite *merenda,* or snack, growing up. He loves it hot or at room temperature. If you like, serve the chicken pieces over a salad of arugula, tomatoes, and onions.

Italian recipe name: *Milanese di Pollo*

Preparation time: *15 minutes*

Cooking time: *10 minutes*

Yield: *4 servings*

Special tools: *Plastic wrap, meat pounder, paper towels, aluminum foil*

1½ pounds chicken cutlets (4 cutlets)

Salt and pepper to taste

2 eggs

½ cup flour

½ cup flour

3 cups fresh bread crumbs, or 1 cup dry bread crumbs

2 cups peanut oil

1 Place each chicken cutlet between 2 large sheets of plastic wrap and pound them with a meat mallet (or the bottom of a heavy pan if you don't have a mallet) until they're evenly about ¼-inch thick. Lightly season with salt and pepper.

2 In a medium bowl, lightly beat the eggs. Generously season with salt and pepper.

3 Spread the flour over a large plate. Spread the bread crumbs over another plate.

4 In a skillet large enough to hold 2 of the cutlets (use 2 pans, if necessary), heat half the oil over medium heat for about 4 minutes. Don't allow the oil to smoke. Evenly coat 2 chicken cutlets with flour, shaking off the excess. Dip them, 1 at a time, in the eggs, letting any excess drip off. Then dip them in the bread crumbs, lightly shaking them to remove the excess. Slip the chicken cutlets into the skillet, making sure that they don't overlap.

5 Cook the cutlets for 2 to 3 minutes on one side, or until they're a rich golden brown. Turn and cook until browned on the other side, another 2 to 3 minutes. Transfer the chicken cutlets to a platter lined with paper towels and gently pat the top with paper towels. Loosely cover with foil to keep the chicken warm while you repeat this procedure with the 2 remaining cutlets.

Breaded Chicken Cutlets in Tomato Sauce

For this dish, breaded chicken cutlets are pan-fried and then simmered in a tomato sauce flavored with garlic, anchovies, and capers.

Italian recipe name: *Panate di Pollo Rifatte*

Preparation time: *15 minutes*

Cooking time: *30 minutes*

Yield: *4 servings*

¼ cup olive oil

3 cloves garlic, peeled and chopped

Pinch of hot red pepper flakes

8 anchovy fillets, chopped

½ cup white wine

3½ cups (28-ounce can) plum tomatoes

¼ cup capers, drained and chopped

1 cup chopped fresh parsley (about 1 large bunch), or ¼ cup dried parsley

Salt and pepper to taste

Breaded Chicken Cutlets, Milan Style (refer to recipe earlier in this chapter)

1 In a medium skillet, heat the olive oil, garlic, and red pepper flakes over medium heat. Cook until the garlic just starts to brown, 2 to 3 minutes. Add the anchovy fillets and wine, cooking until the wine reduces by half. Add the tomatoes and capers and simmer for 10 minutes. Then stir in the parsley and simmer for another 5 minutes. Adjust the seasoning with salt and pepper. Set aside.

2 Prepare the chicken cutlets. Add the cooked cutlets to the sauce and simmer for 5 minutes. Serve.

Chicken Cutlets with Spinach

This dish is especially light and delicious.

Italian recipe name: *Pollo alla Fiorentina*

Preparation time: *10 minutes*

Cooking time: *30 minutes*

Yield: *4 servings*

3 tablespoons olive oil

4 cloves garlic, peeled and crushed

1½ pounds chicken cutlets (4 cutlets)

Salt and pepper to taste

Juice of 1 lemon (about 3 tablespoons)

1 cup white wine

2 cups cooked fresh spinach, or 10-ounce package frozen spinach (thawed and drained)

14-ounce can plum tomatoes or 1 cup Tomato and Basil Sauce

1 In a large skillet, heat the olive oil and garlic over medium heat. Cook until the garlic just starts to brown, 2 to 3 minutes. Season the chicken cutlets with salt and pepper and add them to the pan. Cook until lightly browned on 1 side, 2 to 3 minutes. Turn the cutlets over and cook for another 2 minutes. Then drain any fat from the pan. Add the lemon juice and wine and continue cooking until the liquid has reduced by three-fourths, about 5 minutes.

2 Stir in the spinach and cook for 3 minutes. Add the tomatoes and simmer for 10 minutes. Adjust the seasoning with salt and pepper and serve.

Chicken Cutlets with Artichokes

Starting with canned artichokes hearts rather than fresh artichokes saves a tremendous amount of prep time. Serve this dish as is or use the chicken and artichokes as a sandwich filling.

Italian recipe name: *Scaloppine di Pollo con Carciofi*

Preparation time: *15 minutes*

Cooking time: *30 minutes*

Yield: *4 servings*

2 cloves garlic, minced, plus 2 cloves garlic, peeled and crushed

2 tablespoons chopped fresh parsley, or 2 teaspoons dried parsley

1 medium tomato, diced

Two 8-ounce cans artichoke hearts, drained

Salt and pepper to taste

¼ cup olive oil

1½ pounds chicken cutlets, pounded (4 cutlets)

¼ cup flour

Juice of 1 lemon (about 3 tablespoons)

1 cup white wine

1 Preheat oven to 375°.

2 In a medium bowl, combine the minced garlic, parsley, tomato, and artichoke hearts. Season with salt and pepper. Mix. Set aside.

3 In a large oven-safe skillet, heat the olive oil and crushed garlic over medium heat. Cook until the garlic just starts to brown, 2 to 3 minutes. Season the chicken with salt and pepper and lightly dust them with flour. Place them in the skillet and cook until lightly browned on one side, 2 to 3 minutes. Turn the cutlets over and cook for another 2 minutes. Then drain any fat from the pan. Add the lemon juice and wine and continue cooking until the liquid has reduced by three-fourths, about 5 minutes.

4 Stir in the artichoke mixture and cook for 3 to 4 minutes. Adjust the seasoning with salt and pepper. Cover the skillet and transfer it to the oven. Cook for 10 minutes. Serve the cutlets.

Chicken Cutlets with Tomato and Basil Salad

This summer dish features grilled chicken breasts served with a salad of chopped tomatoes, cucumber, bell peppers, and herbs. Cutlets will stick to a dirty grill, so make sure to scrape the grill thoroughly just before cooking the chicken.

Italian recipe name: *Battuta di Pollo dell'Estate*

Preparation time: *15 minutes (plus 30 minutes marination time)*

Cooking time: *10 minutes*

Yield: *4 servings*

Juice of 1 lemon (about 3 tablespoons)

¼ cup plus 1 tablespoon olive oil, divided

Salt and pepper to taste

1½ pounds chicken cutlets, pounded (4 cutlets)

1 medium tomato, chopped

1 small onion, finely sliced

1 yellow bell pepper, seeded and finely sliced

1 small seedless cucumber, diced

½ cup chopped fresh basil, or 1 tablespoon dried basil

2 sprigs fresh oregano, or 2 teaspoons dried oregano

2 tablespoons red wine vinegar

1 Preheat grill to medium-high.

2 In a medium shallow baking dish, combine the lemon juice, 2 tablespoons olive oil, and salt and pepper. Mix to combine. Place the chicken in the dish, turning the cutlets over a few times to evenly coat them with the marinade. Cover and refrigerate at least 30 minutes.

3 In a large bowl, mix together the tomato, onion, yellow pepper, cucumber, basil, oregano, vinegar, and the remaining 3 tablespoons olive oil. Season with salt and pepper.

4 Place the chicken on the grill and cook for 1½ minutes. Rotate each cutlet 90 degrees and grill for another 1½ minutes. Turn the cutlets over and repeat on the other side. Check to make sure that the cutlets are cooked through. If they need to cook further, move them to a cooler part of the grill, cover, and grill for another 1 to 2 minutes. Transfer the chicken to the bowl with the vegetables. Mix and serve.

Chapter 8

• • • • • • • • • •

Meat: Where's the Beef?

In This Chapter

• • • • • • • • • • • • • • • • •

▶ Buying meat with confidence

▶ Handling and cooking meat safely

▶ Choosing the right cut

• • • • • • • • • • • • • • • • •

Most Italian meat dishes are fairly simple. Presumably, everyone has already eaten an antipasto and a first course. Often, the pasta or risotto is fairly rich and contains many different flavors. Meat dishes tend to be on the plain side—some breaded cutlets sautéed in oil and served with lemon wedges or perhaps a loin of pork roasted with garlic and rosemary.

Unlike many other European cuisines, Italian cookery generally presents meat dishes without complicated or heavy sauces. Many dishes are served with their own juices as a "sauce." When sautéing cutlets or scaloppine, you make quick pan sauces by adding wine or stock to the browned bits left in the pan after you've cooked the meat.

Traditionally, most Italian homes couldn't afford large quantities of meat. So Italians served meat in small quantities, after pasta, risotto, polenta, or soup. Since the end of World War II, Italy has become a wealthy country, and Italians now eat meat in larger portions. The recipes in this chapter reflect these newer eating habits and suit most American tastes.

Cooking meat

Chefs may be able to tell when a piece of meat is done by touch, but the rest of us need some other clues. You can cut into meat and see what it looks like, but this is very imprecise and causes precious juices to be lost. We recommend that you cook meat by internal temperature.

If you pick up an instant-read thermometer at your local kitchen shop for $10, the days of overdone beef or pork will be over. When you think the meat might be done, simply stick the end of the thermometer deep into the meat (away from any bones and fat which can distort the reading) and wait about 10 seconds for the temperature to register. If the meat is not up to temperature, remove the thermometer and try again in a few minutes. Instant-read thermometers will be destroyed if left in an oven for more than a minute or two, so remember to pull them out of the meat before you close the oven door.

Residual heat will cause the internal temperature of large cuts to rise by another 5° as the meat rests on the counter before carving. Even the internal temperature of steak will jump several degrees from the time you take if off the grill to the time you sit down to eat. If you want your beef cooked to 140°, pull it off the heat after the internal temperature reaches about 135°. Note that instant-read thermometers do not work with really thin cutlets. Measuring the internal temperature of cooked meat is easy. Determining what temperature is right for you is another matter.

Health officials recommend cooking all meat until it is well-done. All bacteria is killed when meat is cooked to an internal temperature of 160°. This is not a problem when preparing poultry because poultry tastes best when well-done. However, a steak cooked to 160° is well-done and dry.

Here's the Beef

Grilled Steak, Florentine Style

In Tuscany, steaks are generously coated with salt and pepper before grilling. Besides adding flavor, the salt and pepper form a crisp crust that contrasts nicely with the tender interior of the meat. T-bone steaks are the most commonly grilled cut in Florence. After the steaks are grilled, the meat is removed from either side of the bone and sliced across the grain into thin pieces. You can serve these steaks this way or choose smaller rib eye or strip steaks and serve 1 to a person. Serve the steaks with a side of Stewed Beans with Tomatoes, Sage, and Garlic or Sautéed Broccoli Rabe.

Italian recipe name: *Bistecca alla Fiorentina*

Preparation time: *5 minutes*

Cooking time: *20 minutes*

Yield: *4 servings*

1 tablespoon salt, divided	*4 strip or rib eye steaks (about 14 ounces each), or 2 T-bone or porterhouse steaks (about 1½ to 2 pounds each)*
Pepper to taste	

1 Preheat the grill to high.

2 When the grill is very hot, generously season the steaks with salt and pepper on 1 side only. Place the seasoned side of the steaks on the grill. Do not move them for 3 minutes; then turn them 90 degrees. When the first side is done, about 8 minutes for medium-rare and 11 minutes for medium (depending on the thickness of the steaks and the heat of the grill), season the top of the steaks and flip them over. Cook the steaks 4 to 6 minutes on the second side to desired doneness. Remove from heat and serve.

Beef Strips with Garlic and Rosemary

This recipe is similar to a Chinese stir-fry, except with Italian seasonings and a hot skillet rather than a wok. The "sauce" in this recipe is white wine, most of which cooks off in the pan. Serve with roasted potatoes and salad or use the strips to make great steak sandwiches.

Italian recipe name: *Straccetti di Manzo con Aglio e Rosmarino*

Preparation time: *5 minutes*

Cooking time: *5 to 7 minutes*

Yield: *4 servings*

2 pounds beef (loin, sirloin, or tenderloin), sliced ⅛-inch thick x ½-inch wide x 3-inches long

8 cloves garlic, peeled and sliced

2 sprigs fresh rosemary, or 1 teaspoon dried rosemary

5 tablespoons olive oil, divided

Salt and pepper to taste

¾ cup white wine

1 In a large bowl, combine the beef, garlic, rosemary, 2 tablespoons olive oil, and salt and pepper. Marinate in the refrigerator for up to 6 hours if you have the time or cook immediately.

2 In a large skillet, heat the remaining 3 tablespoons olive oil over high heat. When hot, add the beef and cook, stirring occasionally, for 2 to 3 minutes.

3 Add the wine. Stir to dissolve any flavorful particles on the bottom of the skillet. Cook for 2 to 3 minutes, adjust seasoning, if necessary, and serve.

Meat Loaf, Tuscan Style

This is not your mother's meat loaf. Two miniature meat loaves are browned in a skillet and then simmered in a white bean stew. Cooking the meat loaves in a tomato-flavored bean stew keeps them especially moist and stretches a pound of ground beef to make 4 generous servings. This is a typical Jewish recipe from Tuscany, although the addition of grated cheese is a modern, non-Jewish addition.

Italian recipe name: *Hamim alla Toscana*

Preparation time: *15 minutes*

Cooking time: *1 hour, 45 minutes*

Yield: *4 servings*

½ cup olive oil, divided

1 medium onion, chopped

3 cloves garlic, peeled and chopped

½ cup white wine, divided

4 medium ripe tomatoes, chopped

½ pound dry cannellini beans, soaked overnight in cold water and drained

2 quarts water

Salt and pepper to taste

1 pound ground beef

2 eggs

2 tablespoons grated Parmigiano-Reggiano

3 tablespoons flour

2 tablespoons bread crumbs

1 tablespoon chopped fresh parsley, or 1 teaspoon dried parsley

2 teaspoons chopped fresh sage, or 1 teaspoon dried sage

2 sprigs thyme, chopped, or 1 teaspoon dried thyme

1 cup chicken or beef stock

1 Heat ¼ cup olive oil in a large saucepan over medium heat. Add the onion and garlic and cook until golden, about 3 minutes. Add ¼ cup wine, the tomatoes, beans, water, and salt and pepper. Simmer until the beans are tender but still firm, 50 minutes to 1 hour.

2 In a large mixing bowl, combine the beef, eggs, Parmigiano-Reggiano, flour, bread crumbs, herbs, and salt and pepper. With your hands, work the ingredients together to form 2 equal-sized loaves.

3 In a medium skillet over medium-high heat, heat the remaining ¼ cup olive oil. (If you're using a nonstick skillet, you can use less oil.) Brown the meat loaves on each side, about 3 to 4 minutes per side. Drain the fat from the pan. Add the remaining ¼ cup wine and let it reduce for several minutes. Add the stock and let it cook for 15 minutes.

4 Add the meat loaves to the beans and simmer for 15 to 20 minutes. Slice the meat and serve with the beans.

Roast Beef in Bread Crust

For this unusual recipe, a roast is seared to brown the exterior and then wrapped in uncooked focaccia dough. The roast is then placed in the oven and baked. The result is a tender, juicy roast covered by a golden-brown bread crust. If you have ever had beef wellington, the effect is the same, except focaccia dough is used instead of pie pastry in this recipe.

Italian recipe name: *Arrosto di Manzo Cotto nel Pane*

Preparation time: *30 minutes*

Cooking time: *1 hour, 40 minutes*

Yield: *6 servings*

¼ cup plus 2 tablespoons olive oil

3½-pound boneless beef rib eye roast

Salt and pepper to taste

2 cups white wine

4 cloves garlic, peeled and chopped

2 sprigs fresh rosemary, or 1 teaspoon dried rosemary

2 sprigs fresh thyme, or 1 teaspoon dried thyme

Flour for dusting work surface

1 recipe Everyday Focaccia

1 egg, beaten

1 Preheat oven to 375°.

2 In a large skillet, heat the olive oil over medium heat.

3 Season the rib eye with salt and pepper and add it to the skillet, searing until it is evenly browned, 3 to 4 minutes per side.

4 Drain the fat from the pan and add the wine. Cook for 18 minutes. Transfer the meat to a platter and allow it to cool. Rub the meat with the garlic and herbs.

5 On a flat flour-dusted surface, roll out the focaccia dough until it is large enough to completely cover the roast. Wrap the dough around the roast so that the edges of the dough meet. Trim away any excess. Brush the beaten egg along the edges to seal them. Place the dough-wrapped roast in a baking pan, seam side down, and brush the surface with the remaining beaten egg. Make three or four ½-inch holes in the top of the crust to allow steam to escape. Bake 50 to 60 minutes. Insert an instant-read thermometer in 1 of the holes. When the roast reaches the desired temperature, the meat is ready. If the focaccia begins to brown before the meat is at the desired temperature, turn the oven down to 325° and cook to desired doneness. The crust should be golden brown. Let the roast sit for at least 10 minutes before serving. Slice and serve.

Stew basics

In general, Italian beef is not as tender as beef from the United States. That's why many Italian recipes call for cooking the beef in liquid to make stews or braises.

To make a stew or braise, the meat is seared and then cooked in liquid in a covered pan. This cooking method allows the frugal cook to buy a cheap, tough cut and turn it into something tender and delicious. Most stew recipes start on top of the stove. However, after the meat has been browned and all the ingredients have been added, the pot is usually covered and placed in the oven, where the heat attacks the pot from all sides and ensures that the bottom does not burn.

Most stew recipes will taste even better the next day. Simply cool the stew and refrigerate right in the pot. The next day, skim off any fat that has congealed on the top of the stew and place the pot over a low burner or reheat the stew in a 300° oven until bubbling.

Beef Stew

This recipe demonstrates the Italian cook's ability to turn cheap, tough beef into something delectable. This stew is fairly brothy, so serve it with lots of bread or maybe some mashed potatoes.

Italian recipe name: *Spezzatino di Manzo*

Preparation time: *20 minutes*

Cooking time: *4 hours, 10 minutes*

Yield: *6 servings*

½ cup olive oil

3 pounds beef stew meat, trimmed and cut into 2-inch cubes

Salt and pepper to taste

2 cups red wine

3 medium onions, sliced

3 carrots, sliced

2 celery stalks, sliced

6 garlic cloves, peeled and roughly chopped

2 sprigs fresh rosemary, or 1 teaspoon dried rosemary

2 sprigs fresh sage, or 1 teaspoon dried sage

5 cups water or beef stock, divided

2 cups chopped tomatoes, canned or fresh (optional)

1 Preheat oven to 350°.

2 In a large ovenproof casserole, heat the olive oil. Season the meat with salt and pepper and then add it to the casserole. Brown over medium heat and then add the wine, stirring to dissolve any bits adhering to the bottom and sides of the pan. Let it reduce for 2 to 3 minutes over high heat.

3 Add the vegetables and herbs, reduce the heat, and simmer, covered, for 10 minutes.

4 Add 2½ cups water or stock, bring it to a simmer, cover, and then place the casserole in the oven. Cook for 1 hour, stirring occasionally. Add 1 cup water and the tomatoes (if using), season with salt and pepper, and cook for another 2 hours. Add the remaining 1½ cups water as necessary to keep the stew moist. The meat will be fork tender when done. Adjust the seasoning with salt and pepper, if necessary, and serve.

Braised Beef with Vegetables and Red Wine

For this recipe, you will need a covered pan that can accommodate the meat in a single layer. The pan must also go from the stove top, where the meat is seared, to the oven, where it cooks in a mixture of red wine, tomatoes, and vegetables for several hours. A Dutch oven or round casserole with ovenproof handles or knobs should do the job.

Italian recipe name: *Brasato al Barolo*

Preparation time: *25 minutes*

Cooking time: *3 hours, 40 minutes*

Yield: *4 to 6 servings*

Special tool: *Food processor*

½ cup olive oil

3 pounds beef stew meat, trimmed and cut into 2-inch cubes

Salt and pepper to taste

2 cups red wine

3 medium onions, sliced

3 carrots, sliced

2 celery stalks, sliced

6 garlic cloves, peeled and roughly chopped

2 sprigs fresh rosemary, or 1 teaspoon dried rosemary

2 sprigs fresh sage, or 1 teaspoon dried sage

5 cups water or beef stock, divided

2 cups chopped tomatoes, canned or fresh (optional)

1 Preheat oven to 350°.

2 In a medium, oven-safe casserole or Dutch oven, heat the olive oil over medium heat.

3 Season the meat with salt and pepper and add it to the casserole. Brown the meat on all sides, cooking it over medium-high heat 3 minutes on the first side, 3 on the opposite side, and 1 minute on each of the 2 remaining sides.

4 Drain the fat and add 2 cups wine. Simmer for 10 minutes; add the onions, celery, carrots, garlic, rosemary, and spices. Cook, stirring, for 5 minutes. Add 1 cup wine. Simmer for 5 minutes, cover the casserole, and transfer it to the oven. After 20 minutes, turn the roast, and add the remaining 1 cup wine and the tomatoes. Cook, covered, for 2½ hours, adding a ¼ cup water as necessary to keep the roast moist.

5 Remove the vegetables and juices from the casserole and place them in the bowl of a food processor. Puree. Pour the puree over the roast, cover the casserole, and cook for 20 minutes in the oven.

6 To serve, slice the meat and spoon the sauce over it.

Braised Oxtail

The Italian name of this Roman dish loosely translates as "oxtail, butcher's style." Your average supermarket may not carry oxtail, but most butchers do. When oxtail is braised, it makes an especially hearty and delicious stew.

Italian recipe name: *Coda alla Vaccinara*

Preparation time: *15 minutes*

Cooking time: *3 hours, 25 minutes*

Yield: *4 servings*

¼ cup olive oil

10 cloves garlic, peeled and crushed

5 pounds oxtail, cut into 2-inch pieces

Salt and pepper to taste

2 tablespoons red wine vinegar

2 medium red onions, sliced

2 carrots, cut into ¼-inch pieces

1 cup sliced mushrooms

3 celery stalks, cut into ¼-inch pieces

1 cup red wine

2 ounces pancetta or sliced Canadian bacon, cut into 2-inch squares

4 cups canned whole tomatoes, crushed

2 teaspoons unsweetened cocoa powder

¼ cup water (as needed)

1 Preheat oven to 350°.

2 In a large, oven-safe skillet, heat the olive oil and garlic over medium heat until the garlic begins to brown, about 3 minutes.

3 Season the oxtail with salt and pepper and add the pieces to the skillet. Cook over medium-high heat, turning them occasionally so that they brown evenly. Drain the fat from the skillet, add the vinegar, onions, carrots, mushrooms, and celery, and cook, stirring, for 2 minutes.

4 Stir in the wine and pancetta. Cover and transfer to the oven. After 15 minutes, add the tomatoes and cocoa. Cook, stirring occasionally, for 3 hours; the meat should be fork tender. Add water in ¼ cup increments as needed to keep the stew moist.

The Deal on Veal

Veal has gotten a bad rap. No one wants to think about baby calves, separated from their mothers, locked in cages, and then force-fed milk laced with antibiotics. Unfortunately, that's the way some veal has been produced in the United States.

In the past decade, a more politically correct form of veal has caught on with chefs and consumers. Young calves—veal comes from calves less than four months old—are allowed to graze in fields. This veal, which is called grass-fed, farm-raised, or natural veal, does not have the milky white color of the meat from calves that are caged. The color is rosy, almost like beef. Because these animals are allowed to exercise, the meat is not quite as tender either. However, many chefs believe the flavor is stronger and more interesting.

Caged calves are not much of an issue in Italy. Most Italians are happy to eat veal without questioning how the animals are raised. For the sake of authenticity, buy milk-fed veal. It's certainly easy enough to find. However, if you have given up veal because of concerns about how the animals are raised, you may want to consider the alternative. Grass-fed veal is becoming increasingly available. Many supermarkets, especially those dedicated to natural foods, carry it on a regular basis.

Breaded and Fried Veal Chops

This dish from Milan makes a complete meal with breaded and pan-fried veal chops with a tomato and arugula salad. Rib chops may be used, but loin chops contain a juicy piece of tenderloin that the rib chops don't have and are preferred here.

Italian recipe name: *Lombatina Milanese*

Preparation time: *20 minutes*

Cooking time: *10 minutes*

Yield: *4 servings*

4 boneless veal loin chops, cut 1-inch thick (about 2 pounds total), lightly pounded

Salt and pepper to taste

1 egg

1 cup packaged, dry bread crumbs

1 cup flour

1 cup peanut oil

4 cups arugula

½ cup chopped tomato

1½ tablespoons capers, drained

1½ tablespoons red wine vinegar

¼ cup olive oil

1 tablespoon finely chopped shallots

1 lemon, quartered

1 Trim the chops of excess fat. Cut 3 shallow notches into the outer edge of the meat of each chop to prevent them from curling during cooking.

2 Rub salt and pepper into the veal chops.

3 In a shallow bowl, lightly beat the egg. Spread the bread crumbs in an even layer on a plate. Spread the flour on a separate plate. One by one, flour each chop, dip into the egg, and then roll in the bread crumbs, evenly coating the meat and shaking off any excess.

4 In a large skillet over medium heat, heat the peanut oil. When it is hot, add the veal chops. Cook for 4 to 5 minutes, until golden brown, and then turn and cook for another 4 to 5 minutes. The meat should be almost firm when pressed with a finger. Transfer the chops to a plate lined with paper towels to drain. Repeat this procedure with the other pounded chops.

5 In a large bowl, mix together the arugula, chopped tomato, and capers.

6 In a small bowl, whisk together the vinegar with salt and pepper to taste. Whisk in the olive oil and chopped shallots. Pour the dressing over the salad and mix well.

7 Place a veal chop on each plate and top it with a quarter of the salad. Serve each with a wedge of lemon.

Veal Chops with Tomato Sauce and Mozzarella

For this dish, veal chops are cooked with the flavors of a pizza—tomatoes, basil, and mozzarella—hence the name "pizzaiola." The chops are seared, simmered in a quick tomato sauce, topped with mozzarella cheese, and then baked just until the cheese has melted. Serve with bread to sop up any extra sauce.

Italian recipe name: *Cotoletta alla Pizzaiola*

Preparation time: *20 minutes*

Cooking time: *25 minutes*

Yield: *4 servings*

4 veal loin or rib chops (about 8 ounces each)
Salt and pepper to taste

1¼ cups Tomato and Basil Sauce, or 1¼ cups chopped fresh tomatoes

2 tablespoons flour

1 teaspoon chopped fresh oregano

6 tablespoons olive oil

8 ounces mozzarella cheese, cut into small cubes

6 cloves garlic, peeled

½ cup white wine

1 Preheat oven to 400°.

2 Season the veal chops with salt and pepper and then dredge them in flour, shaking off any excess so that they are just dusted.

3 In a large, oven-safe skillet, heat the olive oil. Add the garlic and cook until it just begins to brown. Add the veal chops and cook over medium heat for 5 minutes; then turn them and cook for 3 to 4 minutes on the other side. Drain the fat from the skillet. Add the wine, cooking until it almost all evaporates. Then add the Tomato and Basil Sauce and oregano. Simmer for 5 minutes. Sprinkle the mozzarella cheese over the veal chops and transfer the skillet to the oven. Bake for 8 to 10 minutes, until the cheese is bubbly.

Venetian Style Calf's Liver

Slow-cooked onions are the secret to this recipe from Venice. Italian cooks use veal stock, but at home you can use chicken stock.

Italian recipe name: *Fegato alla Veneziana*

Preparation time: *20 minutes*

Cooking time: *40 to 45 minutes*

Yield: *4 servings*

⅓ cup plus 1 tablespoon olive oil, divided

4 medium onions, sliced

Salt and pepper to taste

1¼ pounds calf's liver, cut in
2-inch x ½-inch slices

½ cup flour

2 bay leaves

½ cup red wine

3 tablespoons white wine vinegar

½ cup chicken stock

1 In a medium skillet, heat the olive oil over medium heat until hot. Add the onions, season with salt and pepper, and cook, covered, stirring frequently, until the onions are soft, about 25 minutes. Lower the heat if the onions begin to brown.

2 Place a strainer over a bowl and spoon in the onions. Let them drain for a few minutes. Set the onions aside and pour the drained oil back into the skillet.

3 Sprinkle the liver slices with salt and pepper and lightly dust them with the flour.

4 Heat the oil in the skillet and add the remaining 1 tablespoon olive oil, liver, and bay leaves. Cook, stirring occasionally, until the meat is lightly browned, 5 to 6 minutes. Add the wine and vinegar. Cook for 2 to 3 minutes; add the stock and return the onions. Cook for another 5 to 7 minutes. Serve.

TOQUE TIP

The skinny on scaloppine

Thin veal cutlets, called *scaloppine* in Italian or scallops in English, are the most versatile veal cut. These thin pieces can be sautéed in just a few minutes. Like chicken cutlets, they are appropriate with dozens of pan sauces. They are outrageously expensive, but veal lovers seem willing to pay the price.

Ideally, scaloppine should be cut across the grain of the top round. Cut this way, the scallops won't buckle or bend in the pan, and the entire cutlet will brown. If the surface of the cutlet is smooth, it has been cut across the grain. A bumpy or irregular surface that looks like lines indicates that the cutlets have been cut improperly.

Veal scallops should be pounded thin, either by the butcher or by you. At home, you can place the scallops between two pieces of wax paper or plastic wrap and use a meat mallet or the bottom of a heavy pan to flatten them. Ideally, the cutlets should be about ¼-inch thick after pounding.

Veal Scaloppine with Lemon and Wine

Serve the veal with sautéed spinach and Mashed Potatoes.

Italian recipe name: *Picata di Vitello*

Preparation time: *15 minutes*

Cooking time: *15 minutes*

Yield: *4 servings*

¼ cup olive oil

1½ pounds veal scallops, thinly pounded

Salt and pepper to taste

½ cup flour

Juice of 1 lemon (about 3 tablespoons)

1 lemon, thinly sliced

2 tablespoons capers, drained

1 cup white wine

½ cup chicken stock

2 tablespoons chopped fresh parsley

1 In a large skillet, heat the olive oil over medium heat. Season the veal scallops with salt and pepper and dredge them in the flour, shaking off any excess. When the oil is hot, add the veal scallops to the pan. Sauté them for 2 minutes or until they are golden brown; then flip them and brown the other side for another 2 minutes. Drain the oil and discard it.

2 Add the lemon juice, lemon slices, and capers. Mix well and cook for 1 minute. Then add the wine. Cook for 2 to 3 minutes. Transfer the veal to a serving plate. Add the chicken stock to the skillet and cook for 2 minutes. Stir in the parsley and adjust the seasoning with salt and pepper, if necessary. Spoon the sauce over the veal.

Veal with Marsala Sauce

The Marsala wine highlights the sweetness of the veal in this fast sauté. Serve with Sautéed Broccoli Rabe and Mashed Potatoes.

Italian recipe name: *Scaloppine al Marsala*

Preparation time: *10 minutes*

Cooking time: *10 minutes*

Yield: *4 servings*

1½ pounds veal scallops, thinly pounded	*1 cup Marsala wine*
Salt and pepper to taste	*½ cup chicken stock*
½ cup flour	*1 tablespoon chopped fresh parsley*
¼ cup olive oil	

1 Season the veal scallops with salt and pepper and dredge them in the flour, shaking off any excess.

2 In large skillet, heat the olive oil over medium heat. When it is hot, add the veal scallops. Sauté them for 2 minutes or until they are golden brown; then flip them and brown the other side for another 2 minutes. Drain and discard the oil.

3 Stir in the Marsala and cook for 2 minutes. Add the chicken stock and parsley and flip the veal over again. Cook for another 1 to 2 minutes. Transfer the veal to serving plates. Reduce the sauce to the desired consistency and spoon it over the veal.

Veal with Sage and Prosciutto

For this Roman dish, veal scallops are rolled with a slice of prosciutto and fresh sage, secured with a toothpick, and then cooked in a lemon and white wine sauce. The name "saltimbocca" translates as "jump into the mouth," something these tasty veal scallops will surely do.

Italian recipe name: *Saltimbocca alla Romana*

Preparation time: *25 minutes*

Cooking time: *10 minutes*

Yield: *5 servings*

Special tool: *Toothpicks*

1½ pounds veal scallops, thinly pounded (15 scallops, each 2 to 3 inches in diameter)

Salt and pepper to taste

½ cup flour

8 thin slices prosciutto, cut to fit the scallops

15 sage leaves

¼ cup olive oil

½ cup white wine

Juice of ½ lemon (about 1½ tablespoons)

½ cup chicken stock

1 Season the veal scallops with salt and pepper and dredge them in the flour, shaking off any excess.

2 Place a piece of prosciutto and a sage leaf in the center of each piece of meat. Roll the scallops tightly and secure them with toothpicks.

3 In a medium skillet, heat the olive oil over medium heat. When it is hot, add the scallops. Cook for 2 minutes. Then turn them over and cook for another 2 minutes. Drain and discard the oil.

4 Pour the wine and lemon juice into the skillet and swirl to combine. Cook for 2 to 3 minutes, until the liquid reduces by half. Add the stock and cook for another 2 minutes. Using tongs, place three veal scallops on each plate. Reduce the sauce to the desired consistency (it should thicken slightly) and pour it over the veal.

Braised Veal Shanks

This hearty winter dish starts with veal shanks, round pieces of meat about 2 inches thick with a large bone in the center. The shanks are braised for several hours to make them extremely tender. Serve the shanks and their sauce with Mashed Potatoes or Saffron Risotto, Milan Style. Many Italians consider the marrow—the gelatinous material inside the bone—to be a delicacy. If you like, give each person a small cocktail fork or demitasse spoon so that they can pull out the cooked marrow when they have eaten all the meat off the bone.

Italian recipe name: *Osso Buco*

Preparation time: *20 minutes*

Cooking time: *2 hours, 25 minutes*

Yield: *4 servings*

2 tablespoons chopped fresh rosemary, or 2 teaspoons dried rosemary

2 tablespoons chopped fresh sage, or 2 teaspoons dried sage

4 cloves garlic, peeled and chopped

Salt and pepper to taste

4 meaty veal shanks, each about 2 inches thick

1 cup flour

⅔ cup olive oil

1½ cups white wine, divided

2 medium onions, chopped

3 medium carrots, cut into 1-inch pieces

3 stalks celery, cut into 1-inch pieces

4 cups water or chicken stock

3 cups canned plum tomatoes, crushed

1 Preheat oven to 350°.

2 In a medium bowl, mix together the rosemary, sage, garlic, and salt and pepper.

3 Cut 2 to 3 slits in the top of each veal shank and stuff them with the herb/garlic mixture.

4 Season the shanks with salt and pepper and dredge them in flour. Shake off any excess.

5 In a medium, ovenproof saucepan, heat the olive oil over high heat. Add the shanks, browning them well on all sides. Drain and discard any oil remaining in the saucepan. Then add 1 cup wine, stirring to dissolve any bits that have stuck to the bottom of the pan. Add the onions, carrots, and celery. Cover the pan and reduce the heat to medium. Cook, stirring occasionally, for 8 to 10 minutes, and then add the remaining ½ cup wine. Boil the wine for 2 to 3 minutes. Then add the water and tomatoes. Stir well, bring to a simmer, cover, and then transfer to the oven. Cook for 2 hours, stirring occasionally, until the meat is fork tender. Adjust the seasoning with salt and pepper, if necessary, and serve.

On the Lamb

Although lamb looks a bit like beef, it has a much more assertive flavor that works well with a variety of seasonings. Some people shy away from lamb because they think that it is too strong. Good lamb is flavorful and rich, but not off-putting.

If you have had a bad experience with lamb, there are two possible reasons:

- ✔ Lamb fat has a very potent flavor, so make sure to trim away all visible fat before cooking lamb.

- ✔ As lamb gets older and bigger, the flavor can get quite strong. After a sheep turns two, the meat is called mutton. In general, young lamb, slaughtered at around six months, has the sweetest, most delicate flavor.

To judge slaughter age at the market, look at the size. A leg of lamb that weighs 10 pounds invariably has come from a much older animal than a leg that weighs 6 pounds.

Braised Lamb Shanks

The shin portion of the leg is cut into round pieces with meat around the edges and a portion of bone in the center. Like other shanks, lamb shanks will soften only after prolonged cooking. Juniper berries, which are sold in the spice aisle at many supermarkets, give the sauce a pleasant resinous flavor. Serve with Stewed Beans with Tomato, Sage, and Garlic or Lentil Stew or with Basic Polenta.

Italian recipe name: *Stinco d'Agnello*

Preparation time: *10 minutes (plus 1 to 2 hours for marination)*

Cooking time: *2 hours, 20 minutes*

Yield: *6 servings*

6 small lamb shanks, about 12 ounces each

½ cup olive oil, divided

2 cloves garlic, peeled and crushed, divided

2 teaspoons chopped fresh rosemary, or 1 teaspoon dried rosemary, divided

1 teaspoon chopped fresh thyme, or ½ teaspoon dried thyme, divided

Salt and pepper to taste

½ cup flour

1 carrot, peeled and sliced into ¼-inch pieces

2 stalks celery, cut into 1-inch pieces

1 red onion, cut into large chunks

5 juniper berries

1¾ cups white wine

1 cup tomato puree

2 cups beef or chicken stock, divided

1 A few hours before cooking the lamb, rub it with ¼ cup olive oil, 1 clove garlic, 1 teaspoon rosemary, and ½ teaspoon thyme. Season with and salt and pepper. Cover and refrigerate for 1 to 2 hours.

2 Preheat oven to 350°.

3 In a large ovenproof pan, combine the remaining ¼ cup olive oil, 1 clove garlic, 1 teaspoon rosemary, and ½ teaspoon thyme and heat over medium heat for about 1 minute. Coat the shanks with flour, shaking off the excess. Increase the heat to medium-high and brown the shanks on all sides. Transfer the shanks to a plate and set aside.

4 Pour out the excess fat from the pan and add the carrot, celery, and onion. Sauté for 5 minutes, stirring often, and then return the shanks to the pan. Mix well. Add the juniper berries and add more salt and pepper if necessary. Stir in the wine, tomato puree, and 1 cup stock. Bring the mixture to a simmer, cover, and transfer to the oven.

5 Bake for 2 hours, turning the shanks every 20 minutes so that they cook evenly. Add the remaining 1 cup stock as needed to keep the liquid halfway up the sides of the meat. The meat will be fork tender when done; if it is still tough, bake another 30 minutes.

Lamb with Olives

In Italy, this dish is often served with Basic Polenta and Sautéed Broccoli Rabe. The bitter greens contrast nicely with the sweet, salty lamb.

Italian recipe name: *Agnello con le Olive*

Preparation time: *10 minutes*

Cooking time: *2 hours, 40 minutes*

Yield: *4 servings*

⅓ *cup olive oil*

6 cloves garlic, peeled and sliced

Pinch of hot red pepper flakes

2 sprigs fresh thyme, or 1 teaspoon dried thyme

2 pounds lamb shoulder, trimmed and cut into 2-inch cubes

Salt and pepper to taste

Juice of 1 lemon (about 3 tablespoons)

1 cup white or red wine

2 cups canned plum tomatoes, chopped

2 cups water or broth

1 cup pitted olives

1 In a medium, oven-safe saucepan, combine the olive oil, garlic, red pepper flakes, and thyme. Sauté over medium heat, stirring, for 5 minutes.

2 Season the lamb with salt and pepper and add it to the saucepan. Cook, stirring occasionally, for 10 to 15 minutes, until the lamb has released its juices.

3 Add the lemon juice and wine and boil for 3 to 5 minutes. Add the tomatoes, cover the pan, and simmer for 1 hour, stirring occasionally. Then stir in the water and cook another hour at a gentle simmer. Add more liquid (water or broth) as needed to keep the stew moist during the last hour of cooking. Add the olives and cook for 15 minutes. Adjust the seasoning with salt and pepper and serve.

Cooking Today's Leaner Pork

Few fresh products have changed as much over the past 50 years as pork. At one time, a single pig generated 50 or 60 pounds of lard when it was brought to market. Breeding and leaner feeds have really slimmed down pigs. Now the average pigs yields just 8 pounds of lard at slaughter. Talk about a diet that works!

No one really misses all that lard. But these leaner pigs are yielding remarkably leaner cuts of pork. In the old days, overcooking pork was hard to do. Internal fat was in abundant supply, and the fat kept basting the meat as it cooked.

Marketers try to convince us that pork is the "other white meat." They point out that pork has almost as little fat as chicken. What they won't tell you is that pork cooked the old-fashioned way will be dry and tough. These leaner cuts must be cooked differently.

Cooking pork with plenty of liquid is one way to keep it from drying out. But don't overcook pork. Many old-time recipes call for a final internal temperature of 180°. Pork cooked this way will be about as juicy as shoe leather.

Roast Pork Loin

To keep pork loin, which is a relatively lean cut, from drying out in the oven, it is roasted in lots of olive oil. When the roast is almost done, the oil is discarded. Given the large quantity of oil used in this recipe, you may want to economize by using pure olive oil.

To turn this into a complete meal, add several quartered potatoes to the roasting pan about 45 minutes before the roast is done. The potatoes will cook in the fat in the pan and become especially delicious.

Italian recipe name: *Arista alla Toscana*

Preparation time: *25 minutes*

Cooking time: *2 hours*

Yield: *6 servings*

6 cloves garlic, peeled

3 sprigs fresh rosemary, or 2 teaspoons dried rosemary

1 tablespoon salt

½ tablespoon pepper

4 pounds pork loin (with bone)

1½ cups olive oil

1 cup white wine

1 Preheat oven to 400°.

2 On a cutting board, chop together the garlic, rosemary, and salt and pepper. Mix well.

3 With a sharp knife, make narrow slits 2 inches deep in the meat. Stuff the slits with the garlic mixture. Massage any leftover garlic mixture into the meat. Place the pork loin in a roasting pan. Pour the olive oil over it and roast, uncovered, for 20 minutes.

4 Turn the roast and lower the oven temperature to 325°. Roast another 40 minutes. Add the wine. Cook for another hour, turning at 20 minute intervals. Drain and discard the oil. Let the meat rest for 5 minutes before carving.

Sautéed Pork Chops with Tomatoes and Olives

Chops come from several places on the pig. Center loin and center rib chops are meatier and not as chewy as sirloin and blade chops.

Italian recipe name: *Bistecchine di Maiale in Padella*

Preparation time: *10 minutes*

Cooking time: *35 minutes*

Yield: *4 servings*

4 pork chops, about 8 ounces each

Salt and pepper to taste

¼ cup olive oil

5 cloves garlic, peeled and crushed

2 sprigs fresh rosemary, or 1 teaspoon dried rosemary

½ cup white wine

1½ cups chopped plum tomatoes (fresh or canned)

½ cup pitted black olives

1 Season the pork chops with salt and pepper.

2 In a large, nonstick skillet, heat the olive oil over medium heat. Add the pork chops, garlic, and rosemary. Gently shake the skillet to distribute the oil under and around the pork and then cook for 5 to 6 minutes without turning. Turn the chops over and cook the other side for 5 more minutes. Drain and discard any fat from the skillet.

3 Add the wine, allow it to boil for about 5 minutes, and then transfer the pork chops from the skillet to a large plate.

4 Add the tomatoes to the skillet, season with salt and pepper, and simmer for 10 minutes. Return the pork chops to the skillet and add the olives. Cook, covered, for another 5 minutes. Place a pork chop on each plate and top with the tomato/olive sauce.